V. S. PRITCHETT

A Study of the Short Fiction

Also available in Twayne's Studies in Short Fiction Series

Samuel Beckett: A Study of the Short Fiction
    by Robert Cochran

Jorge Luis Borges: A Study of the Short Fiction
    by Phyllis Lassner

Kay Boyle: A Study of the Short Fiction
    by ELizabeth S. Bell

John Cheever: A Study of the Short Fiction
    by James O'Hara

Gabriel García Márquez: A Study of the Short Fiction
    by Harley D. Oberhelman

John Gardner: A Study of the Short Fiction
    by Jeff Henderson

Graham Greene: A Study of the Short Fiction
    by Richard Kelly

Ernest Hemingway: A Study of the Short Fiction
    by Joseph M. Flora

Katherine Mansfield: A Study of the Short Fiction
    by J. F. Kobler

Flannery O'Connor: A Study of the Short Fiction
    by Suzanne Morrow Paulson

Liam O'Flaherty: A Study of the Short Fiction
    by James M. Cahalan

John Steinbeck: A Study of the Short Fiction
    by R. S. Hughes

Peter Taylor: A Study of the Short Fiction
    by James Curry Robison

Robert Penn Warren: A Study of the Short Fiction
    by Joseph R. Millichap

William Carlos Williams: A Study of the Short Fiction
    by Robert Gish

Virginia Woolf: A Study of the Short Fiction
    by Dean Baldwin

Twayne's Studies in Short Fiction

Gordon Weaver, General Editor
Oklahoma State University

V. S. Pritchett in 1988. Photograph © Jerry Bauer

V. S. PRITCHETT

A Study of the Short Fiction

John J. Stinson
SUNY College at Fredonia

TWAYNE PUBLISHERS • NEW YORK

Maxwell Macmillan Canada • Toronto

Maxwell Macmillan International • New York Oxford Singapore Sydney

Twayne's Studies in Short Fiction Series, No. 37

Twayne Publishers   Maxwell Macmillan Canada, Inc.
Macmillan Publishing Company   1200 Eglinton Avenue East
866 Third Avenue   Suite 200
New York, New York 10022   Don Mills, Ontario M3C 3N1

Macmillan Publishing Company is a part of the Maxwell Communication Group of Companies.

Library of Congress Cataloging-in-Publication Data

Stinson, John J.
    V. S. Pritchett: a study of the short fiction / John J. Stinson.
       p. cm. — (Twayne's studies in short fiction ; no. 37)
    Includes bibliographical references and index.
    ISBN 0-8057-8341-5 (alk. paper)
    1. Pritchett, V. S. (Victor Sawdon), 1900– —Criticism and
interpretation. 2. Short story. I. Title. II. Series.
PR6031.R7Z88 1992
823'.912—dc20   92-1337
                                        CIP

For Dianne, with love

Contents

Preface   xi
Acknowledgments   xvii

PART 1. THE SHORT FICTION

The Early Years   3
Major Accomplishment   19
Assured and Unhurried Artistry   40
The Old Master   55
The Writer's Palette   73
Pritchett's Achievement   77
Notes to Part 1   84

PART 2. THE WRITER

Introduction   89
Interview, 1975   90
   Douglas A. Hughes
"The Writer's Tale"   102

PART 3. THE CRITICS

Introduction   107
Douglas A. Hughes   108
Eudora Welty   122
William Trevor   127

Chronology   131
Bibliography   134
Index   144

Preface

V. S. Pritchett is a novelist, critic, travel writer, short-story writer, and one of the most highly praised literary autobiographers of the century. Ironically, it is probably his versatility, for a period now extending beyond 60 years, that causes many people ordinarily quite knowledgeable about contemporary literary history to have a somewhat blurred idea of who he is. That Pritchett should be so relatively poorly identified by the reading public is surprising, in that reviewers and members of the literary establishment generally consider him the best short-story writer and popular critic writing in England today.

While professional writers and editors have held Pritchett in high esteem for quite some time, scholars and critics, somewhat like readers at large, have had their attention diffused by the multiplicity of his writing talents. A further reason for the inattention is that Pritchett's greatest accomplishment is in the short-story form, a form that until recently has suffered the curious fate of general neglect. Until the 1980s not a single article in a scholarly or literary journal, nor even a short chapter in a book, was devoted exclusively to Pritchett's short fiction. Other modern British and Irish masters of the short-story form—writers like A. E. Coppard, H. E. Bates, Sylvia Townsend Warner, Mary Lavin, and William Trevor—have suffered the same fate. The resurgence of interest in the short-story form has begun to supply the remedy for the neglect of Pritchett. In 1982 a French academic, Alain Theil, familiar with the theories of Todorov and Barthes, published a 376-page study of Pritchett's short fiction. *Les Nouvelles de V. S. Pritchett* (in French except for quotations from Pritchett) is slow, careful, and methodical, but the essential Pritchett, elusive of all critics, seems largely to slip through Theil's nets of theory. Dean R. Baldwin's 1987 *V. S. Pritchett*, the first book on the author in English, is, like Pritchett's own criticism, sensibly astute, most intelligently selective, and a model of clear, graceful, and economical writing. Readers interested in the totality of Pritchett's achievement should go immediately to Baldwin's book; although a pioneering work, it is not likely soon to be surpassed as a general introduction.

One has to admit, however, that despite Baldwin and Theil, and such fervent advocates as Frank Kermode, Walter Allen, and Paul Theroux, Pritchett may be a writer who will not live on, the criterion supplying the doubt being the minute representation his stories have received in college anthologies. Baldwin begins the last paragraph of his book with a remark on the "subtle and elusive" quality of Pritchett's stories, and it is precisely this elusiveness—the lack of a sufficient number of clear interpretive clues—that renders the stories resistant to New Critical dissection.

Interpretation of Pritchett stories is sometimes frustrated because causality is dim or ambiguous. Pritchett himself has warned that "the intellectual must face causality; but he had better remember casuality and the inexplicable."[1] In fact, most Pritchett stories seem to be wafted away in the wind as heavy critical machinery is driven up. Largely absent in them are symbolic patterns of imagery, strong organization on principles of binary opposition, and other avenues favored by explicators. One critic observes that "his world is too uncomplicated; . . . every problem seems to vanish."[2] Another reviewer feels that "in Pritchett's stories nothing is ever quite resolved; indeed, having come full circle, his situations seem to dissolve at the very place where they began."[3]

✛

In part 1 of this volume I make some brief comments about Pritchett's life in relation to his fiction. My emphasis is always on the artistry of each individual story, but if a known biographical fact seems to provide genuine illumination, I mention it. Because the biographical comments I sometimes weave into the discussions are more easily understood when readers have a basic knowledge of the main points of Pritchett's life, I will provide here a very quick sketch. Readers wishing to know more should consult the two eminently readable volumes of autobiography—*A Cab at the Door* (1968) and *Midnight Oil* (1971)—or Baldwin's study.

Victor Sawdon Pritchett was born near London, in Ipswich, Suffolk, on 16 December 1900. His father, Walter Sawdon Pritchett, originally a Yorkshireman, was a traveling salesman; his mother, Beatrice Martin Pritchett, was a Cockney shopclerk, one of the London poor. Walter Pritchett was a man much like Mr. Micawber of Dickens's *David Copperfield;* his absurd social aspirations, confused romanticism, strutting mannerisms, pumped-up optimism, and domestic tyranny created strong impressions, and, later, confusion and exasperation in his children. Walter converted to and warmly embraced the religion of Christian Science when Victor was a boy. Although Victor quite consciously set himself on very different paths from those of his father, it seems clear that his father's was the most profound single influence on his life. The vainglorious Walter Pritchett is, quite transparently, the prototype of major characters in several stories, but his influence on his son's fiction goes well beyond these guest appearances. Other important influences on the young Victor were his mother's tall stories, the family's constant moving from place to place (18 separate moves alone from the time Victor was born until he was 12), and his early reading of Dickens.

When Victor was not quite 16 his father removed him from school and sent him to work in the leather trade in London, where he was to remain for four years. At age 20 he made a courageous break to Paris, learned French, worked at low-paying jobs, imbibed the Parisian atmosphere, nearly starved to death, read widely in French and English literature, and began his career as a writer. He sold pieces to two British weeklies and a series of illustrated articles to the *Christian Science Monitor*. In 1922 the *Monitor* hired him (although he was a lapsed Christian Scientist) as a correspondent and sent him to Ireland to report on the civil war. In Ireland Pritchett filed his reports, attended the Abbey Theatre, met Yeats and O'Casey, and married an Irish actress. In the beginning of 1924 the *Monitor* sent him to Spain, where he again soaked in atmosphere and learned a new language; from there it dispatched him to North Africa, the United States, and back to Ireland before firing him in 1927. Although Pritchett and his wife did not legally divorce until 1936, their marriage fell apart, for reasons Pritchett does not specify, somewhere during those years.

Back in London in 1927, Pritchett supported himself by working as a librarian and by writing stories and sketches, and then conceived the idea of walking across Spain to gather material for an original travel book. Published in 1928 as *Marching Spain*, Pritchett's first book brought him favorable attention. It was followed a year later by an unsuccessful novel, *Clare Drummer*. Undeterred, Pritchett embarked in earnest on the short-story career that I describe in the rest of this book, and published his first collection, *The Spanish Virgin*, in 1930. Just a few years later his passionate love relationship with Dorothy Roberts, whom he married in 1936, stimulated him to increased artistic productivity. He continually testifies that she was and is a constant source of happiness, security, renewal, and fulfillment.

✦

For various reasons I have made neither extended nor even highly concentrated attempts to trace all possible literary influences on Pritchett, a writer who has often "confessed" to having read a great amount. More important than influences is his achievement of a sharp and highly distinctive personal voice in his fiction, and in fact he recommends that other practitioners cultivate a unique voice. He said in an interview that "the short story writer is like someone who sings a song. The singer has his own voice. It isn't the voice of anyone else."[4] William Peden, an authority on the development of the short story, notes that "despite his early acknowledged indebtedness to Hemingway and others, Pritchett was his own man, finding his own way, his own material, his own forms."[5]

In his fiction as in his life, Pritchett has been a writer who has kept himself free of coteries and claques. Walter Allen, the prominent and sensible British critic, maintains that "in whatever genre he writes, [Pritchett] is always *sui generis*."[6] Paul Theroux, the American novelist, critic, and travel writer, writes that "the stories seem to have no echoes or influences."[7] The truth seems to be—not so very different from what these critics maintain—that the influences on Pritchett are so varied, so subtle, and so heavily refined that any effort to discuss patterns of influence would be a large and amorphous enterprise, one entailing a rehearsal of much of the history of the short story. Charles Dickens, Anton Chekhov, Guy de Maupassant, H. G. Wells, Robert Louis Stevenson, James Joyce, G. K. Chesterton, Ernest Hemingway, D. H. Lawrence, Anatole France, Isaak Babel, Pio Baroja (a not very widely known Spanish writer), Katherine Mansfield, A. E. Coppard, and Liam O'Flaherty have all, with varying degrees of plausibility, been suggested (mostly by reviewers) as influences on Pritchett's short stories. Pritchett, an ardent watercolorist as a young man, may very well have been influenced by impressionist painting, although in a way far less obvious than, say, Virginia Woolf. It may be even more sensible to claim that cross-influences exist between Pritchett's work and that of H. E. Bates and Sylvia Townsend Warner, and that he has influenced the English (but not the Irish) stories of William Trevor and has possibly had some influence on Angus Wilson. In part 1, then, I mention possible influences only when the evidence seems compelling.

Space limitations make it impossible to discuss all 82 of the *Complete Collected Stories* or the uncollected stories. I comment on those stories I deem most artistically successful, or most illustrative of certain themes, techniques, or critical problems associated with Pritchett's stories. I discuss a few stories—"Sense of Humour," "It May Never Happen," "The Sailor," and "The Saint"—at greater length than others not simply because they are the best known but because they most clearly exemplify certain essential characteristics. In part 1's penultimate chapter I briefly categorize Pritchett's major themes and mention stories not previously dealt with; interested readers can take off from a few hints and immediately establish thematic patterns and parallels.

I approach the stories chronologically rather than thematically in the first four chapters so that readers who wish to find a unified critique of a particular story need only consult the Index. Some of the story references in the Index will lead the reader to Pritchett's own remarks about his stories—in Douglas A. Hughes's illuminating interview with him and in Pritchett's pithy essay "The Writer's Tale," both reprinted in part 2. In part 3 the reader will find a perceptive original essay by Hughes and incisive and beautifully articulated review essays on Pritchett's stories by two distinguished practitioners of the short-story form: Eudora Welty and William Trevor.

Wherever in part 1 it seems useful or appropriate I intertwine commentary about Pritchett's developing craft, his characteristic themes and techniques, and the merits and dangers of certain of his forms and styles with my discussions of the individual stories that most seem to call for some broadening of the particular to encompass the general. We are still in the beginning stages of Pritchett studies; numerous analyses and syntheses will doubtless follow of the writer whom a prominent English reviewer calls "the best living English short story writer"[8] and whom Walter Allen considers the most "outstanding English short-story writer ... since the death of D. H. Lawrence" (Allen, 268). If in this book I hope to convince readers of anything it is only that Pritchett's stories, infused with artistry and cunning that are products of both intuition and careful discipline, will be the source of pleasure, fascination, and profitable scholarly study for years to come.

✦

Except for stories specified in the notes to part 1, in-text page references are to *Complete Collected Stories* (New York: Random House, 1991).

Notes

1. John Mellors, "V. S. Pritchett: Man on the Other Side of a Frontier," *London Magazine*, April/May 1975, 10.
2. Matthew Hodgart, *New York Review of Books*, 20 March 1975, 32.
3. Susan Heath, *Saturday Review/World*, 19 October 1974, 29.
4. Douglas A. Hughes, "V. S. Pritchett: An Interview," *Studies in Short Fiction* 13 (Fall 1976): 426.
5. William Peden, "V. S. Pritchett," in *The English Short Story, 1880–1945*, ed.

Joseph M. Flora (Boston: Twayne, 1985), 150.

6. Walter Allen, "V. S. Pritchett," in his *The Short Story in English* (New York: Oxford University Press, 1981), 268; hereafter cited in text.

7. Paul Theroux, "V. S. Pritchett's Stories: His Greatest Triumph" (review of *Collected Stories*), *Saturday Review*, May 1982, 56.

8. Valentine Cunningham, "Coping with the Bigger Words" (review of *Collected Stories*), *Times Literary Supplement*, 25 June 1972, 687.

Acknowledgments

Permission has been kindly granted to quote from the following works:

Complete Collected Stories by V. S. Pritchett, copyright © 1947, 1949, 1956, 1959, 1960, 1961, 1962, 1966, 1967, 1973, 1974, 1979, 1982, by V. S. Pritchett. Reprinted by permission of Random House, Inc.

"V. S. Pritchett: An Interview" by Douglas A. Hughes, *Studies in Short Fiction* 13 (Fall 1976): 423–32. © 1976 by Newberry College. Reprinted by permission of Newberry College.

"The Writer's Tale" by V. S. Pritchett, *Vogue*, March 1981, 327–28, 362. © 1981 by V. S. Pritchett. Reprinted by permission of Sterling Lord Literistic, Inc.

"A Family of Emotions" by Eudora Welty, *New York Times Book Review*, 25 June 1978, 1, 39–40. © 1978 by The New York Times Co. Reprinted by permission of the *New York Times*.

"Pritchett Proclaimed" by William Trevor, *New Republic*, 2 August 1982, 30–32. © 1982 by The New Republic, Inc. Reprinted by permission of the *New Republic*.

I am grateful to several people for various kinds of assistance. Dennis Vannatta and William Peden caused a deepening of my interest in the short story. I profited greatly from reading Dean R. Baldwin's *V. S. Pritchett* in Twayne's English Authors Series, and I found the interview and several essays in the special V. S. Pritchett issue of the *Journal of the Short Story in English* (Spring 1986) to be profitable. The editors, Gordon Weaver of Oklahoma State University and Liz Traynor Fowler of Twayne, provided friendly guidance and encouragement. I wish to thank SUNY College at Fredonia for a "released time" grant and particularly James Shokoff for the remarkably constant and always friendly support of his faculty. I am indebted once again to both the Reference and Interlibrary Loan Divisions of Reed Library of SUNY College at Fredonia. My deepest thanks are reserved for my wife, Dianne, not simply for patience, encouragement, and secretarial assistance but also for reading all of Pritchett's stories and engaging me in animated and challenging conversation about them.

Part 1

THE SHORT FICTION

The Early Years

"Sense of Humour" and the Pritchett "Problem"

"Sense of Humour," the first story in *Complete Collected Stories*, provides an excellent place to begin this study. Pritchett's signature voice and approach are amply present here, whereas they were yet to be discovered in the earlier stories, which deserve only brief comment. But like other of his best work, often the title stories of collections—"It May Never Happen," "When My Girl Comes Home," and "The Camberwell Beauty"—"Sense of Humour" causes doubt and uneasiness in the minds of critics. How else are we to explain not simply the absence of critical commentary but the exclusion from virtually every college anthology of this and all other Pritchett stories, whether highly successful or mediocre? The case is intriguing because, to a number of writers and reviewers—Margaret Drabble, Frank Kermode, Walter Allen, Paul Theroux, Robertson Davies, Eudora Welty, and William Trevor among them—Pritchett is *the* great English short-story writer of our time.

The answer to the question of Pritchett's neglect is obvious, remarkable only for its not being specifically remarked on after all these years. Simply put, it is that Pritchett provides fewer interpretive clues than most writers; consequently, neither critics nor general readers can arrive at tidily definitive interpretations of many of his stories. Pritchett's stories may be seen, in New Critical parlance, as inchoate or lacking in sufficient organic unity. Even if we allow for tensions and functional ambiguities, a few necessary clues (formal, symbolic, textural) will seem to be missing or to point in the wrong direction. Epiphanic moments are just as apt to bathe characters and readers in murky as in revealing light. While no critic focuses directly on these problems, Anatole Broyard seems to have something like it in mind as he querulously asks, "If one gave Mr. Pritchett the benefit of the doubt, if one assumed that his untidy stories cohered in some roundabout way, what then? Even if they worked, they would not be enough."[1]

Readers will probably be more disconcerted by interpretive difficulties in Pritchett's stories because they are unsignaled: Pritchett is not thought to be anywhere near the cutting edge of experimentation, the place most readers identify with interpretive difficulty. They generally expect interpretive clear sailing in a Pritchett story when they note no fragmentariness, no twisted chronologies, no elaborately selfconscious plays with point of view, no formal obliquities of an obvious sort ("When My Girl Comes Home" being the single large exception). In a number of Pritchett's most important stories, they will meet what a leading theorist, Austin M. Wright, terms "mimetic resistance": some "unresolved contradiction at the level of character or action."[2] Pritchett's various kinds of openness are, in one argument, not readily accepted or understood because short-story theory is not at a sufficiently sophisticated point of development to be able to describe or classify them. Nevertheless, Pritchett's methods are not all that surprising, in that suggestiveness, implicitness, and indirection are the characteristic ingredients of the twentieth-century short story, and irony that of modern literature generally. In his own unfussy, unprogrammatic sort of way Pritchett carries these tendencies to the limit and in so doing demands much from both reader and critic.

Pritchett's is the art of severe selectivity. But his artful trick is to employ a rigorous selection while seeming to allow the story to unfold naturally, even casually. Pritchett, who acknowledges a general Hemingway influence, is, in a less obvious way than Hemingway, Stein, or Fitzgerald, his own kind of "leaver-outer." In the preface to his *Collected Stories* Pritchett writes of his typical procedure of "boiling down a hundred pages into twenty or thirty."[3] This process of composition through excision gives rise to what we might call Pritchett's "haze effect," the sense that his characters, like figures in great Russian novels, or like people in real life who are not family members or intimate friends, seem surrounded by a haze that hides the edges of their personalities. The excisions affect the plot as well: unity becomes equivocal; how exactly the pieces of the plot hang together becomes problematic. Vagaries of plot, character, or structure seem designed, in Pritchett's best-known stories, to compel readers to engage in some ruminative reflection.

✦

"Sense of Humour," Pritchett's first major story, the one he says signaled that he "had modestly arrived,"[4] both teases and entertains. Pritchett, whose remarks in interviews or autobiography are not guilefully calculated to self-advertise his stories' depths or dimensions, has simply labeled it "a piece of premature black comedy" (*MO*, 126). It is that, but it is also a good deal more.

Readers of moderate sophistication will realize that the first-person narrator, who is also one of the story's two chief characters, can be trusted in the facts he reports but cannot be trusted in his judgments or ways of "seeing": his moral perceptions and ordinary human sensibilities have been severely dulled by a rigid, puritanical background that places its emphases on money, getting ahead, frugality, appearances, and respectability. Although Pritchett deals gently and compassionately with his characters and lacks the moral indignation of the satirist, his stories frequently carry a sting when they deal with people like this narrator, Arthur Humphrey, a commercial traveler whose type can be recognized in an American counterpart, the Willie Loman of his early and middle years. They form a series of hypocritical or morally obtuse members of the middle-class business community, people whose ordinary humanity has been twisted and severely diminished by adherence to such pervasive doctrines as that which views earthly prosperity as a harbinger of salvation.

As the story begins, Arthur informs the reader he is working a new sales territory for the first time. He does not wait for Monday morning, because he wants to attend two different churches on Sunday in the first town: "it pays in these small towns to turn up at church on Sundays, Presbyterians in the morning, Methodists in the evening" (1), he says. From this alone readers might be led to view Arthur as a caricature out of the fiction of a Sinclair Lewis. But the story is not just a satiric cartoon or a black comic sketch; its sharply and cannily observed social details, rendered with all the right nuances, almost dare the reader to question why it should not be thought of as social realism. After all, the Arthur Humphreys of the real world are not only not obliterated by satire but hardly ever seem even to recognize themselves.

Readers can note the unerringly accurate ear for the speech of people of different social classes that Pritchett had developed by this time. In *Midnight Oil* Pritchett says, apropos "Sense of Humour," "I think ... that I gave the vernacular of that period a role it had not had up till then" (228). The very first thing the reader of *Complete Collected Stories* encounters is the convincingly realistic sound of Arthur's voice:

> It started one Saturday. I was working new ground and I decided I'd stay at the hotel the weekend and put in an appearance at church.
> "All alone?" asked the girl in the cash desk.
> It had been raining since ten o'clock.
> "Mr. Good has gone," she said. "And Mr. Straker. He usually stays with us. But he's gone."
> "That's where they make their mistake," I said. "They think they know

5

everything because they've been on the road all their lives."
   "You're a stranger here, aren't you?" she said.
   "I am," I said. "And so are you."
   "How do you know that?"
   "Obvious," I said. "Way you speak."
   "Let's have a light," she said.
   "So's I can see you," I said.
   That was how it started. (1)

Using a smooth but aggressive conversational style common to his sort, Arthur soon makes up to the attractive desk clerk at the hotel, Muriel Mac-Farlane. They have some things in common: both have a macabre sense of humor (she attributes hers to being Irish), and both have made frugality a habit. Muriel's boyfriend, Colin Mitchell, a young fellow who works at a nearby garage, is tormented when Muriel goes out with Arthur. When Arthur takes Muriel out in his car, Colin almost always follows them on his motorbike. Arthur says Colin "seems to be a harum-scarum sort of half-wit to me" (5), and Muriel replies, "And he spends every penny he makes" (5). Arthur is blind to Colin's agony, regarding him, because of perceived class difference and Colin's inarticulateness, almost as a creature from another species. "I used to call him 'Marbles' because when he spoke he seemed to have a lot of marbles in his mouth" (6), Arthur tells the reader. Arthur, in a demanding and superior way, confronts Colin about his always following Muriel and him: "'She was my girl' was all he [Colin] said. He was pouring oil into my engine. He had some cotton wool in one hand and the can in the other. He wiped up the green oil that had overflowed, screwed on the cap, pulled down the bonnet, and whistled to himself" (7). Readers will apprehend Colin's suffering far more clearly than Arthur does; by this point in his career Pritchett was handling such dramatic ironies with great confidence and ease.

The relationship between Muriel and Arthur intensifies, and one bank holiday the two of them go for a visit to Arthur's parents' house. While there they receive a telephone call informing them that Colin has just been killed in an accident. He had been trying again to follow them on his motorbike but, passing other vehicles recklessly, had "gone clean off the saddle and under the Birmingham bus. The blood was everywhere. . . . What a mess!" (10). Not surprisingly, one of Arthur's first thoughts is simply "Holiday ruined" (11).

The combination of black comedy and the exposure of moral vacancy and hypocrisy continues to the end of the story. Colin's mother is assisted greatly in the funeral arrangements by virtue of the fact that Arthur's father is an undertaker and has a good eye for business. All quickly arrange to have Colin's body conveyed back to his own town in Colin's father's hearse with, in order to save money, Arthur as the driver. Muriel decides she really ought to be with Colin on this occasion, but it is fairly clear she also wishes to be with Arthur: "'No, no,' she said. 'I want to go with Colin. Poor Colin. He loved me and I didn't love him.' And she drew my hands down to her breasts" (14). She rides in the front of the hearse with Arthur. Arthur thinks about the way Colin always followed behind them, and he is a bit uneasily aware that Colin is still behind them, no longer on his motorbike but now in his casket. Arthur and Muriel feel some awkwardness as they ride, but also a curious sense of satisfaction, almost elation. They like it that men lift their caps respectfully as they drive past in the hearse. The story ends with a broadly ironic remark from Muriel: "Look at that man there. Why doesn't he raise his hat? People ought to show respect for the dead" (17).

The preceding summary is true both to the facts and to the basic tenor of the story. But it does not tell the whole truth about the story, or suggest its complexities. "Sense of Humour" is shaped and controlled, and it provides more of a sense of closure than many Pritchett stories. At its conclusion readers will have a sense of having moved closer to illumination. Still, they will also feel a sense of interpretive irresolution and elusiveness. A resonating core of mystery and complexity is in fact present in many of Pritchett's best stories, and it is this quality that gives them their special character and memorability.

The lifelike complexity of the characters of both Arthur and Muriel accounts for our inability to pin down meaning absolutely, but this indefinite quality produces more satisfaction than frustration. Arthur and Muriel are a good deal more than walking exemplifications of moral vacancy. The remorseless modern business ethic, for example, has not completely suffocated Arthur's humanity. "I felt sorry for that fellow" (7) and "I could have been friends with that fellow" (7) (that is, were they not rivals in love) are Arthur's thoughts before Colin's death—at least as he reports them to the reader. As they ride back in the hearse, Muriel at one point begins to laugh, and Arthur chooses to shut her up: "'Keep your sense of humour to yourself,' I said" (16). This might well be only Arthur's middle-class respectability and hypocrisy at work, but it might also be some submerged sense of decency that is rising.

The story's largest mystery centers on an event that is in itself quite plausible: the first instance of sexual intercourse between Arthur and

Muriel, on the very night of Colin's death. Space does not permit a discussion of the multiplicity of reasons for Muriel's giving herself to Arthur that night or for her repeatedly moaning "Colin, Colin, Colin" (12) even as they made love. Muriel herself probably does not know fully; the pathways of the mind are dark and tangled. Arthur is troubled: "Did she love Colin all the time? Did she think I was Colin?" (12). Readers can devise a scale of motivations for Muriel that range from the morally disgusting to the laudable. On the base end of the scale, she may have calculatedly seized on an opportunity for unprotected sexual intercourse as a means of levering Arthur into marriage. This motivation may seem unlikely, but Arthur is soon thinking that the unexpected sexual activity "had put my calculations out. I mean, supposing she had a baby. You see I had reckoned on waiting eighteen months or so" (15). On the other end of the scale, readers might note that several times Muriel explains her behavior by saying, "I'm Irish. I've got a sense of humour." Such explanations might well mean, as Dean Baldwin suggests, that Muriel "can laugh at herself and the absurdities of human folly,"[5] that she is so fully in touch with the flow of the universe that she is able to accept life fully, and also death, which is but a part of life. Numerous possibilities, of course, exist in the middle of the scale. Commenting on the irreducibly mysterious motivations of Muriel, British reviewer Paul Binding has said that "we are changed—and devoured—by what we are unable to understand.[6]

The interpretive ambiguities are more than a storyteller's tease: they are additional invitations for readers to reexamine the bases by which they define their own moral and psychological lives.

You Make Your Own Life

"Sense of Humour" was the first story of the 1938 volume *You Make Your Own Life*. Although just the second volume of Pritchett's stories, it displayed Pritchett (especially in "Sense of Humour") at a stage close to his mature style. "Sense of Homour," at about 7,200 words, is a medium-length story for Pritchett; one of the other most significant stories of *You Make Your Own Life*, "Handsome Is as Handsome Does," at about 14,000 words, is long. This story of a husband and wife involved in a union that is masochistic but also strongly symbiotic is perceptive, but it is also one of the few successful Pritchett stories in which he explicitly and systematically provides the motivations for his characters. Pritchett has said that he "wrote the story when my first marriage was over, and the character of my first wife was in some ways, but only partially, like that of the woman in the story . . . masochistic, frustrated when very young."[7] The Corams' marriage is characterized by the presence of psychological influences that cause them to maintain a firm sense of alliance even as they feel a constant and fierce opposition to each other. "They were always quarreling" (39), an observant and trenchant third-person narrator informs the reader of this unattractive couple in their forties. Tom, now an industrial chemist, was the son of a man who had a small boot-repairing shop in the Midlands (54–55); Julia's "family were country gentry, not very rich, with small private incomes and testy, tiresome genteel habits" (55).

As readers of English fiction or observers of English life might expect, the difference in class background colors their relationship. Tom, educated out of his own class, has not even come close to feeling socially comfortable anywhere else. He is now lost between classes; he does "not belong anywhere" (55). Utilitarian, parsimonious, and mistrustful of beauty or pleasure, Tom Coram is another of Pritchett's puritans. As a young woman Julia had held herself at a psychological distance from her slightly shabby genteel family; she recoiled from the thought of a marriage to a dull army officer, the norm for a woman of her class and position. She felt herself to be a person cut off, and judged Tom Coram to be someone in the same position. "He was ugly in life, she was ugly in body; two ugly people cut off from all others, living in their desert island" (55) is Julia's own pronouncement to herself on the nature of their union.

The omniscient narrator provides an easy and cogent commentary that is never glib; this is combined with a direct presentation of the thoughts, actions, and reactions of the Corams, particularly Julia. Julia's bitterness and frustration with Tom have been building powerfully over the years. Her sense of grievance is increased by her feeling that their inability to have children is one more deficiency of her husband. Tom is "helpless" (39), boorish, full of ill-focused resentments, inarticulate, and "a man without subtlety or wit" (41). Julia, "a short, thin woman, ugly yet attractive" (38), intelligent, charming, and inquisitive, spends a lot of time "covering" for her husband. Pritchett demonstrates all this by isolating the Corams in a small pension on the French Mediterranean with just the proprietor, M. Pierre, and an urbane and agreeable but somewhat secretive young guest, Alex. Tom's comments are aggressively stupid: he says that what is wrong with the Côte d'Azur is that "there's no industry" (42), and he finds everything associated with the Mediterranean a "fraud," including Pierre's ability to swim.

In actuality, both Pierre and Alex are quite strong swimmers; Tom is the one who can only nervously claw his way through the water for short distances. Symbolically, Tom swims in the same dogged, joyless way he moves through life; Alex and Pierre's buoyancy and sense of ease in the water mirror their more relaxed acceptance of life and its complexities. The story's fulcrum is the near-drowning of the fat, sixtyish Pierre, one of several instances in Pritchett's stories where a near-drowning brings with it a revelation. A strong undertow has pulled Pierre near some rocks, and he is so exhausted that he can neither swim to safety nor pull himself out. Julia begs her husband to do something, but he backs away in cowardly fear. Alex, however, arrives on the scene and, with instinctive heroism and utter disregard for his own life, accomplishes a daring rescue.

For the first time in all their years together, as they ride back to the hotel, Julia does not allow Tom to "escape one moment of her contempt" (69). The nervous energies of the afternoon precipitate a network of confused emotions in Julia, and she attempts a quick seduction of the handsome young Alex in his room. Alex, shocked, rejects her, but she comes to feel she did not really want him for himself anyway. "She had abased and humiliated herself" (71), she sees; it is and always has been in humiliation and abasement that she and Tom are united. She recalls the moments following Alex's rescue of Pierre and remembers that "her desire had not gone winged after the rescuer, but angry, hurt, astounded, and shocked towards her husband" (72). That evening, when she tells the story of the rescue, she makes Tom the hero of the story, not Alex. The bond that tied them has held after all; it is, as the last words of the story have it, "The Corams against the world" (73).

In outline the psychological relationship of Tom and Julia might seem bizarre; within the contours of the story, however, it is convincing. William Peden plausibly notes that the Corams are "what the psychiatrist Edmund Bergler has termed 'injustice collectors,' neurotics who 'suffer from a hidden need to feel that the world has wronged them.'"[8] In the same vein we can also note that Tom, his northern gloom always disposing him to find the pleasures of the world shabby and deceitful, exacts constant punishment on himself. Julia, whom, significantly enough, the narrator always refers to as Mrs. Coram, has come to be her husband's appendage. She chose Tom long ago: she made her bed and must lie in it. She has internalized our culture's deadly judgment that the absence of physical beauty betokens worthlessness; subconsciously she perhaps seeks to punish herself for this worthlessness by staying with Tom. The irony of the story's title is precisely that it does not convey the expected irony: the physically handsome Alex also performs handsomely; the physically unattractive Corams behave unhandsomely. The ending of the story, wherein Julia reports Tom as Pierre's rescuer, suggests that the Corams' relationship has virtually reached the folie à deux, the functional psychological reaction in which two persons who have long been intimately associated come to share the same delusions, usually persecutory ones. Admittedly, Julia seems to *will* herself to share the delusions, and the shimmering core of the story's mystery resides in her, not Tom.

Readers might well reflect that there really are many people like the Corams in the world, or, in a broader generalization, that the submerged motives for husbands and wives staying together are perhaps nearly as many as the submerged motives driving them apart. Something generically human is almost always just beneath the surface of the bizarre or eccentric in Pritchett.

✢

The "material" of "You Make Your Own Life," the title story, also seems bizarre at first, for it involves a murder attempt through poisoning and a man's slitting his own throat. Sensational as these events may seem, it is the unsensational way in which they are related—by one of those most intimately involved—that gives the story its meaning, its flavor, and its memorably effective ironies. Peden briefly notes the Hemingwayesque character of the story, "the brevity, directness, understatement, and effective use of dialogue."[9] But "You Make Your Own Life" is also one of a number of good stories in which the elements of tragedy, comedy, and satire are so closely blended that the reader is virtually compelled to indulge in philosophical ruminations.

Like a better-known story also concerned with small-town life, Ring Lardner's "Haircut," the story proper is contained in a barber's conversation with an out-of-town customer in the chair, but Pritchett, unlike Lardner, uses the customer as a first narrator to provide a small frame and also to ask a few questions. "In a dead place like this town you always had to wait" (150), the customer tells the reader. He is forced to wait because the dandified young man presently in the chair is "having everything" (150).

When the visitor gets into the chair, the barber tells him, in a slightly amused but nonchalant manner, a strange tale concerning himself and the previous customer, Albert, the man who had the "works" but was allowed to leave without being asked to pay. He relates that Albert, some years before, had been suffering from tuberculosis and had been nursed by a young woman, the "prettiest girl in town" (153), for whom Albert soon felt deep pangs of love. Albert tried to put the relationship on an amorous level, despite his awareness that the barber, his best friend, was courting her. The young woman herself felt nothing more than pity for Albert. Albert was desperate enough to try to rid himself of his competitor by murder: he offered the barber a drink from a poisoned bottle of whiskey. Not being a drinking man, the barber refused, and prepared to marry his girl later that same week.

Albert cut his own throat and "called out to a kid in the street to fetch *her*" (155), wanting her to see the "present" he had made for her. But he survived and "got over it" (155), the barber says: "Comes round and plays with my kids on Sundays. Comes in every Friday, gets himself up. See him with a different one every week at the pictures. It's a dead place this; all right in the summer on the river. You make your own life" (155).

What does this relatively brief (about 2,600 words) story "mean"? Readers are left almost entirely to their own devices in determining the exact destination or even direction of the irony. Some readers will judge that the story has no real point, that it is too coy in its handling of ironies, and that the technique of having sensational events related in blasé fashion creates merely bemusement, a poor substitute for meaning. While the observation is only partly illuminating, we can note that Pritchett is often interested in the ways individuals are shaped by their environments; here the barber and Albert are obvious products of the small-town way of life. Albert's adjustment involves a return to more normal rhythms of that life and is consonant with Pritchett's interest, more like that of some novelists, in life's arbitrariness and fluidities—odd, singular, sometimes capricious events that seem not to be a part of any easily discernible pattern. And if Pritchett's plots, mirroring the events of life (some disappointed lovers committing suicide in any town), emphasize contingency, his characters are also often inconsistent, occasionally because of the dynamic nature of the self but more often because of its self-deceiving nature: "I never see people as being consistent within themselves at all,"[10] Pritchett told an interviewer. This vision leads to a wide range of ironies playing illuminatively with ideas about illusion/reality and inner view/outer view.

✦

"The Upright Man," one of the rare Pritchett stories that is almost an allegory, deals with large and significant themes but sacrifices full thematic development for the sake of underscoring some neatly turned ironies and metaphoric correspondences. The story is an angry comment on the mechanical, dehumanizing nature of work in the twentieth century, the hell that is modern warfare, and the relationship between war and work.

Calvert, the protagonist, is a shy, morally upright clerk whose head is always bent to duty. The modern world holds legions of such men: "There were iron bars to the windows of his office. Through them if a bowed man looked up, he saw not the sky but across the street the flat walls of windows where other bowed men worked" (126). Calvert remains the model clerk until one day "the gods, his gaolers, got drunk and went mad" (127). They tell him, "You are a man already. Your pale face is tanned by the sun, your neck is golden. Your hair which has gone dead and greasy is alive again like corn. . . . You're a hero. Go and kill" (127–28). Released from deadly tedium, suffused with new life, standing straight and tall, Calvert and hundreds of thousands of others go "like upright gods" (128) off to war. But "this was a trick. They were made to stand in rows in trenches as they had sat in rows at desks, but the pens they now used required two arms to lift" (128).

Pritchett describes Calvert's war experience in a highly stylized way. It is concentrated and even elliptic; the feelings of Calvert as he is seriously wounded are conveyed with immediacy and economy: "He fell. It seemed he was whipped off his feet while his head peeled like a helpless belfry. Now there was nothing left of him, he was scattered into fragments and flung together in an iron ball of pain, to be struck and struck until he broke into nothing but clangorous and bloody echoes; and then great toothed pliars picked him up by the skull and flung him away down into a black pit that had no end to it and measured only by the wail of his pain as he dropped down" (129).

The narrative voice informs the reader that Calvert has been shot through the neck, and the wound is such that he will never be able to bend his head again. Back home, this once best of clerks is unable to bend his head to clerical tasks; he is now forever an upright man physically, just as he has always been an upright man morally. Someone decrees that he shall be a messenger, and this is what he becomes. Yet, as the story's closing words inform the reader, he is "not a live man, not a dead man, a man now without all means of desiring anything, a man indelibly alone not looking up or down. An upright man" (130).

The story has the air of a parable; the bitter sardonicism of tone in which it is conveyed was, of course, common to much literature of the 1920s that dealt with World War I. This brief story (about 2,100 words) provides effective illustrations of the psychological bases of war and its romanticization. Men spiritually killed by enervating work in which they can take no pride yearn for release, but war turns out, contrary to their expectation, to provide no resurrection. For many, though, it provided another release, death, an end they were perhaps subconsciously seeking, since it is unnatural for the body to survive when no longer invested with spirit. It can be seen that Calvert, although physically alive at both the story's beginning and end, is spiritually dead the whole time. "The Upright Man" deserves to be better known, if only as an effectively compressed record of a common spiritual reaction to World War I.

✦

Readers will expect "The Scapegoat" to be invested with a grave and weighty theme. Its simple rhetoric suggests a folktale; its tone and mood, a political allegory. Its title seems to promise some revelation of a dark underside to a present-day enlightened society. The characters seem to carry vague, atavistic shadows along with them. Because all these elements are present in some way, many readers will be intrigued, but they may also find that the ideas lack sufficiently clear definition and resolution.

The story is set in a working-class neighborhood of London sometime in the period between the world wars. Two adjacent streets, Terence Street and Earl Street, have a long-standing rivalry and enmity. The story's narrator is a denizen of Terence Street, and he tells the story in a way that is apparently candid, yet clearly limited by his own perspective and background. He tells the reader that the people of Earl Street are "a different class of people from ourselves altogether" (105). The two streets are now in a fierce contention to raise more money than the other for the celebration of the "Jubilee" (possibly that of George V in 1935). Terence Street has not got off the mark quickly in its fund-raising effort, because its people are wary of entrusting any individual with a sum far larger than they themselves could save in a lifetime. They finally decide on Art Edwards, a self-effacing widower of regular habits. The responsibility seems to be releasing Edwards from his tendency toward involution, but then, suddenly and shockingly, he loses all the collection money at the dog track, returns home, and promptly hangs himself. The people of Terence Street are first numb and then resentful, but when Earl Street mocks and jeers, Terence Street embraces Edwards as "our hero, our god" (119) who "had borne our sins" (119). They give Edwards an enormous funeral, a "procession . . . a mile long when it got going" (119).

The title obviously leads us to conclude that the story archetypally uses the primitive scapegoat ritual; it in fact does, but few reverberative depths are achieved as a result. An explication notes that "one of the actions present in the primitive scapegoat ritual is the beating or many beatings which precede the victim's expulsion," and that "beatings exist at nearly all levels of importance in the story." This explication also points out that ultimately "the ritual of violence is transcended by the elevation of Art from the role of scapegoat to that of dying god whose death is a prelude to a new life."[11] Although such comments accurately indicate Pritchett's intentions, the correspondences between the primitive ritual and the events of the story seem slightly contrived and mechanical, not really a psychologically effective evocation of the forces of the unconscious.

Some literary works have given us characters that are comic, tragic, satiric, politically allegorical, and archetypal almost all at once (one might think of J. M. Synge's *The Playboy of the Western World* or Joseph Heller's *Catch-22*), but Pritchett's mixture in this story does not quite work. He seems uncertain about whether he wishes to deal with his characters as avatars of deep, universal human experience or as somewhat comic examples of operative mob psychology in the working class. Dean Baldwin's comment on this story is sensible and correct: "Since the story first appeared in the *London Mercury* in 1937, when rumblings of war were already audible, it seems likely that Pritchett intended a political message, although exactly what message he had in mind is unclear" (Baldwin, 56).

✤

"Main Road" is very much a 1930s story of social protest, but it surpasses most proletarian fictions by its economy and intelligent control. The story is simple: two hungry, out-of-work men are tramping across the country, mostly down country lanes, to a place where they hope to find some job. The way in which their hunger, disorientation, frustration, and resentment lead them to a robbery (of a young man who turns out, luckily for them, to himself be a poacher) is conveyed feelingly and largely indirectly. For at least one of the men the robbery will neither lessen the sense of degradation nor restore self-respect; the last sentence of the story tells us that "what he wanted, his tortured hating soul cried out within him, was not food" (30).

✤

"Eleven O'clock" provides a strong reminder that such distinctions as those between the "newspaper short story" and the "artistic short story" are sometimes quite arbitrary. "Eleven O'clock" seems at first reading a quick humorous sketch, very pleasant but not very consequential. A second look reveals that it has some suggestion of depth and that the seeming ease of execution results from a blending of precisely selected description, dialogue, and narrative.

A genial milkman on his route meets a fat, open, generous housewife married to "a cripple" (122), a narrow, punctilious watchmaker. The authorial sympathy with a woman who must suffer a crippled husband may seem shallow and callous, but we should see the husband in much the same way we see Sir Clifford Chatterley—the crippled bodies of both symbolically standing in for hearts and souls crippled by the ethos of business and the machine.

The spontaneous housewife is from the North and has been in the South of England for only seven weeks. She finds herself not "like the people round here" (121); she is "neighbourly" (121) and they are not. (The same North-South contrast is to be found in other of Pritchett's stories.) The milkman too is from the North; he is a short, nondescript man, but there is life and emotion inside him: "there is nothing like a uniform for concealing the soul" (120). The first day the two meet, she is "warm and untidy with cooking" (121) and "her body [seemed] to be laughing at her fatness" (121). Without guile or guilt, she is soon giving of herself as well as her pastries in this warmhearted tale of two people who find, without making much fuss about it, some personal need fulfilled in the other. The milkman and his special customer fulfill their desires many mornings at eleven o'clock, while down below, the milkman's mare satisfies her desire by putting her head over a railing and unabashedly eating the amorous housewife's hedge: "Been getting your greens, haven't you?" (125), the contented milkman asks as he returns to his horse. And the story's last sentence tells us that "he stared at the mare and, bright under their blinkers, he saw the eyes of that cynical animal, secretive and glistening, gazing back at him" (125). Readers have no way of really determining how much cynicism, if any, resides also in the milkman. The narrative voice gives off no detectable tone of disapproval of infidelity, and probably none is present: Pritchett had by this time left behind the strict personal sexual morality he diligently guarded into his twenties.

✛

"A Spring Morning" too is a kind of hymn to the sexual drive, although it also hinges on the ironies of inner view/outer view. It provides a small slice of an eternal drama—the sexual and amorous stirrings of youth in springtime. Pritchett's handling of this material is calculatedly half-ironic, half-celebratory. The boy, an energized mixture of cockiness and uncertainty, smells of motor oil and tobacco; the flirtatious girl, thin and ill-nourished, with two big and protruding front teeth further detracting from her appearance, nonetheless feels herself attractive, and is indeed a vitally attractive force—at least to this one young man, at this particular moment. The story's point is perhaps enhanced by its riding a knife edge between empathy and somewhat cruel condescension. Pritchett does, though, consistently find joy amid shabbiness and frustration.

Conclusion

The stories of *You Make Your Own Life* are thematically and stylistically varied, and somewhat uneven in ambition and merit. In all of them, though, Pritchett displays assured control and good artistic judgment even if, as in "The Aristocrat," he provides only cleverly crafted ironies in the Maupassant mold. The same cannot be said of his first volume of stories, *The Spanish Virgin and Other Stories* (1930), works that are worth mentioning only as testimony to the considerable forward leap in artistry displayed in *You Make Your Own Life*.

When Pritchett made his choice about which of his stories to include in *Collected Stories, Selected Stories, More Collected Stories*, and, finally, *Complete Collected Stories*, he consistently decided to leave unresurrected the stories of *The Spanish Virgin*. Pritchett's choice was an intelligent one: the linea- ments of short-story genius are scarcely discernible in this apprentice volume. Largely absent are Pritchett's subtlety, delicate suggestivity, and relaxed yet thoroughly authoritative control of his material. It is obvious that Pritchett was feeling his way into the form and into the writer's profession. He was doing what he had to do to start himself off as a writer: "I began, in those early days, by writing anecdotal sketches of real people, because the newspapers liked that kind of thing. This taught me to look and listen" (*CS*, x).

Pritchett is perhaps most embarrassed by the title story, a novella of about 24,000 words; it is lacking in proportion and structure, and uncertain of its desired effects. It proceeds episodically, and occasionally relies heavily on melodramatic effects. Remarkably, an anonymous reviewer for the *Times Literary Supplement* gave the volume a flattering review and singled out this story for special praise; the book's modest sales success was probably indebted to this influential review, and perhaps Pritchett's decision to pursue the short-story craft was as well.

Three of the 13 stories—"Tragedy in a Greek Theatre," "The White Rabbit," and "The Cuckoo Clock"—have balance, economy, and no false notes and are modestly successful as a result. Edward J. O'Brien, the American expatriate who helped a number of English short-story writers, selected the first of these—a story whose theme is the near-inevitable contamination of art by commerce—for his *Best Short Stories of the Year* (1927). The latter two stories present two more of the twisted faces of puritanism. These three stories are at least equal in merit to the five or six least consequential stories of *Complete Collected Stories*, but we can understand Pritchett's rationale for excluding them: when he wrote them he "had not yet found a distinctive voice which is indispensable to the short-story writer and the poet" (CS, x).

Pritchett did find that "distinctive voice" in "Sense of Humour," a story that comes close to giving us the essential Pritchett. It was more than fortuitous that that was the first story of Pritchett's second volume, and it is a happy choice that he kept that order in the *Complete Collected Stories.*

Major Accomplishment

By the late 1940s Pritchett, at least in his best stories, was capturing characters of surprising depth and dimension—and capturing them sharply—while seeming to allow them to live and breathe and eventually go on their own way, without giving his reader a sense that these characters had been reduced or violated. Because most short-story writers aspire to this goal, Pritchett's achievement testifies to some success of art or craft but not necessarily to conscious innovation. Pritchett has been generally suspicious of self-conscious experimentation and programmatic movements of any sort in literature. Widely read in Western literatures, he knows that yesterday's fashions in literature are today's clichés or dim memories. For him, what will abide is character.

It May Never Happen

"I think I find the drama in human personality, in character rather than in events,"[12] Pritchett has written. That Pritchett knows character revelation to be his forte can be seen in his choice of stories from *You Make Your Own Life* for inclusion in *Collected Stories*: "Sense of Humour," "Handsome Is as Handsome Does," and "You Make Your Own Life." In their imaginative grasp and their subtle conveyance of the complexity of emotions and the multiplicity of motives within people, these stories rise clearly above the volume's others. They bear markedly strong similarities to the three most noteworthy stories of the next volume, *It May Never Happen*: "The Sailor," "The Saint," and "It May Never Happen." These six early successes are all similar in that they deal with memorably unusual people who nonetheless are invested with full humanity. Five of the six (all but "Handsome Is as Handsome Does") are first-person narratives relying heavily on dialogue, the result of Pritchett's recognition that "I'm so much better at writing dialogue than I am at this awful, elaborate analysis."[13] Four of the six (all except "You Make Your Own Life" and "The Saint") present two round characters involved in a conflictive or complementary relationship with each other.

Reasonably, it seems, both critics and ordinary readers have termed the characters of these six stories (and many other Pritchett stories) "eccentrics." Pritchett has several times objected to that designation: "It has been said that many of my people are eccentrics. They do not seem so to me, but very native English in that they live for projecting the fantasies of their inner, imaginative life and the energies that keep them going. I have always thought it the duty of writers to justify their people, for we all feel that for good or ill, we are exceptional and justified in being what we are" (*CS*, x). I use the term *eccentric* because it is a useful designator and is as reasonably accurate as most such terms are, but I heed Pritchett's caution: the term implies no adverse judgments of his characters; in fact, readers should understand that Pritchett's characters are enacting feelings or hidden impulses closely analogous if not identical to those we all have. Only rarely will Pritchett deny a character an abiding respect, for we are all united in our frail but aspiring humanity. Pritchett writes that the drama of his stories lies "in the absurdities or the pathos of the private imbroglio, . . . in the unconscious self-revelation of people, in the sight of them floundering amid their own words, and performing strange strokes as they swim about, with no visible shore, in their own lives. They are heads sticking out of the water of their own dreams" (*SS*, vi–vii).

The stories of *It May Never Happen* are assured in their techniques, even if those techniques were not the ones provided at the time by books of advice on how to write a short story. That many of these stories strike sudden depths may have something to do with Pritchett's apparent decision that he needed, more than before, to go backward in order to go forward. "I am glad that after thirty I got back into touch with my childhood; this gave me my vocation," he writes in *Midnight Oil* (270). A number of the stories in *It May Never Happen*—"The Lion's Den," "The Saint," "It May Never Happen," "Aunt Gertrude," "The Chestnut Tree," "The Clerk's Tale," "The Fly in the Ointment," and "The Night Worker"—are based on significant personal experiences of Pritchett's early life. In contrast, only two of the stories of the first volume, "The Spanish Virgin" and "The Cuckoo Clock," come out of any early life experience of the author, and no such story appears in the second volume, *You Make Your Own Life*. It is unusual that a writer would wait so long—after all, Pritchett was 45 when this volume was published—to draw artistically on a substantial deposit of perfectly usable personal experience for his short stories.

Pritchett may have thought that large, unrefined chunks of personal experience could not be reduced and made malleable for use in the short-story form, and that he had better reserve them for his longer fiction and autobiography. He was, much later, to achieve consummate success with his two volumes of autobiography, *A Cab at the Door* (1968) and *Midnight Oil* (1971), which many critics rank near the top of the list of twentieth-century autobiographies. He employs his own life heavily but with less success in his 1935 novel, *Nothing like Leather*, which does, however, show an advance over his first two novels.

Of his short stories Pritchett writes that "by the 1930's I had at any rate discovered my voice and that my native bent was to the designs of comedy and its ironies" (*CS*, x). The combined discoveries of voice, métier, and the "right" material (the emotional complexities and strong flavorings of his own early life) were now resulting in Pritchett's producing stories memorable for sharply drawn characters that were odd but—especially with their "real" voices—entirely convincing.

Pritchett's drawing on the "large materials" of his own boyhood and youth produced another fortuitous result. Many of his early stories had been very competent but, with their calculatedly tidy effects, also just a little bit slick. Now as Pritchett struggled to contain materials of a certain magnitude and unruly complexity within the demanding confines of the short-story form, he apparently came upon a method that was to remain with him. Pritchett's method of boiling down material is not quite unique, but it is unusual. Philippe Séjourné was understandably a bit incredulous, as indicated by his good-natured, wondering laugh after putting this question to Pritchett in an interview: "Speaking about your method of working, I was struck by a sentence you use in one of your prefaces, you speak of 'boiling down a hundred pages into twenty or thirty.' Is that what you actually do?"[14] Pritchett responded, "Well I think I actually do" (Forkner and Séjourné, 24–25). He noted that the Russian writer Isaak Babel, whose short stories he finds "quite astonishing," follows the same procedure. The ultimate result of Pritchett's procedure, in the best stories, is that readers are apt to feel a sense of engagement and satisfaction but not the sense of neat resolution that allows them easy disengagement once the story is concluded. The artistry is complete, but inviolable mysteries of personality are carefully preserved.

✦

The title story, "It May Never Happen," exposes some of the teasing ambiguities of real life more than it provides an organic structure of meaning susceptible to fully rewarding analysis. The story's basic situation is not unlike that which the 16-year-old Pritchett encountered when he was sent off to work in the leather trade. This story's narrator is a young man of the same age who takes a job in a London upholstery business in which his earnest Uncle Belton is a partner. Readers of the story soon soak in the atmosphere of the damp, misshapen, sometimes malodorous world of the small but striving commercial enterprise clearly redolent of Dickens. Like Dickens's characters, Pritchett's provide the vivacity and delight of caricature, but Pritchett constantly surprises his readers by allowing meaningful, unmistakable glimpses of third dimensions in characters otherwise seen just as engaging cartoons.

At its deepest level the story is about psychological and spiritual survival in the world of modern business, deadly dull but also menacing. The story follows the reactions of three characters to this world: Vincent, the narrator, an initiate to adult life and the world of the office; Uncle Belton, a relentlessly optimistic businessman like Walter Pritchett; and Mr. Phillimore, Belton's partner, an epicene creature fond of extravagantly proclaiming his weakness and pessimism.

Belton, a kindly but pompous and publicly stern man, has found that his total commitment to the business ethic has provided a haven from psychological storms: "He stepped back from the catastrophic crashes of the inner life. His remedy lay in that part of the Protestant tradition which deals with the conflicts of the inner life by annihilating the inner life altogether" (207). Phillimore, on the other hand, possesses both inner life and mystery. Thirty-five, unmarried, and until recently under the thumb of his mother, Phillimore is a shy man of delicate sensibilities who, despite his shyness, has a habit of verbal effusiveness and an occasional tendency to indulge in theatrical behavior. When Vincent first meets Phillimore he is "startled by a high-pitched, eager feminine giggle" and surprised by his new boss's greeting, "Er—er—hullo, 'ullo, my dear" (204). Phillimore defeats pain and tedium through stylization, dramatization, and even silliness; in this sense he is somewhat like Mr. Pollfax, the comic dentist of "The Oedipus Complex," another story in this volume.

Phillimore is one of those Pritchett characters who soon become compelling because they seem to be composed of contradictory elements. Some will find that the author indulges in the kind of humor that used to be called "wickedly droll" at the expense of a certain type of homosexual; others will not be so sure. What is one to make of the scene in which Phillimore throws himself on Miss Croft, the 17-year-old typist, passionately attempting to kiss her? He declares he loves her (222) and seems to mean it. Is it that he intends only some sort of cruel mockery, despite her affection and respect for him? Or is it that Phillimore has displaced some of the feelings he has for the other young person in the office, Vincent, the narrator? Despite his need for self-dramatization Phillimore is shrewd in his own way and essentially an enigmatic figure. It may be that his dramatic flauntings of his own weakness and delicacy are psychological stratagems to get people to think of everything connected with him as an act, and thus provide a cover for very real weaknesses. But we cannot be sure. Pritchett is fascinated by people's cultivation of public and private selves as distinct from one another, and by the manner in which the two interact. Because we can "know" Phillimore only through Vincent, the narrator, he remains at core unknowable.

When Vincent remarks to the reader that "Nothing happens in an office. One day is like another" (206), he probably expresses the weariness of soul felt by most of those in the office, the weariness that impels Phillimore to enjoy his private ironies and perform his little dramas. But even if Phillimore were not there, one day would not be quite like another. Things appear not to change, but in reality they do. Vincent later notices Miss Croft changing: "what was pretty one week became plain the next. She was like a creature in a chrysalis" (209). Vincent's conception of Mr. Phillimore oscillates as well: usually Phillimore "appeared to put feebleness, illness, fright, incapacity, and failure in life first" (211). He seemed to have "an eagerness to cut a bad figure" (211). At another time Vincent has the impression that "Phillimore was *not* a fool; that he was cunning and obstinate, and longsighted" (212).

Uncle Belton is invested with qualities usually considered masculine. One of Vincent's similes suggests not only the intimidating character of his uncle but a kind of phallic power as well: "he seemed to be shooting upwards at one like a howitzer" (211). Since Phillimore's traits are traditionally thought to be feminine, we might suppose the two men have some sort of complementary relationship. Their business partnership is several times referred to as a marriage, the first time most expressly: "my new Uncle Belton and Mr. Phillimore were husband and wife" (208). But happiness and stability prove elusive in this partnership. Belton and Phillimore intrigue against each other, and each becomes involved in commercial infidelity, forming secret relationships with competitors. The partnership abruptly ends, with Phillimore making a dramatic departure. The movement in the story is a fairly usual one for Pritchett—away from false unity to an open sense of division.

Vincent, in the closing words of the story, tells the reader that

> I saw him once, it must have been eighteen months later. He was standing on London Bridge looking up at a high building where a man was cleaning windows.

"I should die," I heard him say to someone in the crowd. Then he saw me. He bared his teeth as if he were going to spit, but changed his mind. His look suggested that I was the most ridiculous thing on earth, as he turned away. (223)

Despite Pritchett's having chosen "It May Never Happen" as the title story of this important collection, it has received hardly any critical comment, probably because of the paucity of clues that would otherwise allow explicators to arrive at definitive uncoverings of the mysteries of character. (The story's design indeed makes it inadequate to contend that the theme is simply the narrator's initiation into an adult world of moral ambiguity and mystery, and that we should be satisfied with that.) Pritchett's stories resonate all the more, though, when he allows a sizable open place within the walls of the known and the deducible. The question of whether this construction is allowable or illegitimate is complex and goes right to the heart of short-story theory. That said, it must be admitted that critics who might object that Pritchett has simply pared away too much in this story could use as an argument the fact that appearing in Pritchett's novel *Mr. Beluncle* is a character (Mr. Chilly) quite similar to but more clearly defined than Phillimore.

✛

Pritchett again uses retrospective first-person narration and the initiation theme in "The Chestnut Tree," the wistful and humorous story of a 15-year-old office boy at a leather merchants' firm whose experience is much like the author's when young. Some of the boy's co-workers are "characters" and are given a slight "humors" touch; ordinary human beings weighed down by tedium, they occasionally allow themselves a small flourish of personality, producing a pop or two to break the emotional stillness of their day. But the relatively stable office is catalyzed into emotional life by the entry of the first women, two young sisters, both hired as bookkeepers. Sexuality and its concomitant jealousies, suspicions, and competitiveness soon hang heavily in the air, and the strictly raised adolescent reacts with fright, dismay, and disgust even more than with fascination. As in many Pritchett stories, people's instinctive lives, long submerged, briefly break through to the surface and display themselves; most of these people react as a consequence but soon go comfortably back to something very much like their old lives. The sharp, temporary deviations seem, though, to confirm the animal inside the human being inside the clockwork machine.

❖

"The Night Worker," another story that has a basis in Pritchett's early life, is one of the most emotionally moving of an author whose métier is comic irony. In this artful story that deserves to be better known, pathos is the result of reader recognition of the discorrespondence of the inner view/outer view, here of the failure of a young boy to comprehend that he is mostly unwanted by both parents. Pritchett has included the story in *More Collected Stories*, but it has received no critical comment of more than a few words.

A limited omniscient narrator introduces the reader to the focal character, a seven-year-old boy who is frequently sent to his aunt and uncle's house by his parents to get him out of their way. The parents have three other children in the family and another on the way. The boy likes his aunt and uncle, but even more he likes their daughter, his cousin Gladys, a young woman soon to be married. Gladys is spontaneous, good-natured, and optimistic, and she genuinely loves her unwanted young cousin—"nobody's kid" (311) as she refers to him in conversation with Jim, her fiancé.

Much is signified in the story's opening: "A marriage was in the air. In a week the boy's Cousin Gladys was going to be married. The boy sat in a corner of the room out of the way" (306). The imminent marriage creates an aura of joyous excitement that surrounds the boy because he loves his vivacious, good-hearted Cousin Gladys. At the same time, though, he has been both literally and figuratively pushed off into a corner. Although he sleeps in Gladys's room and she calls him "my young man" (307), he will soon be the victim of this marriage because he will be supplanted by Jim. The boy, unnamed in the story and always just referred to as "he," "him," or "kid," is, of course, the victim of another marriage—that of his parents, which resulted in his birth. We witness some sexual byplay between Gladys and Jim and hear some talk about how Jim is a good "night worker"—not just at the post office where he works but in sexual performance with Gladys—which is revelatory of the sexual energy impelling the two toward marriage just as it probably impelled the boy's parents. A sad human cycle of passion, futility, and loneliness seems operative in this working-class milieu.

Pritchett achieves powerful effects in this story by making readers feel the joy of the young couple who are to be married in a few days, while at the same time causing them to be heartbreakingly aware of the pathetic situation of the naive boy, still too young to see things as they are. Prit-

25

chett's emotional modulations are deft, as is his mixture of irony and emotion. The ironies surrounding the boy's failure to comprehend his situation have nothing of the subtleties of James's *What Maisie Knew*, but they are quite believable. And once again Pritchett makes the story more intriguing and realistic by allowing some important openness to remain. For one thing, Jim and Gladys may not repeat the mistakes of the boy's parents: "Can't someone put her wise [sic]" (311), Jim asks about the boy's mother. The conversation of Gladys and Jim even teasingly suggests that either Gladys is pregnant *or* they are seriously considering adopting "nobody's kid." Gladys says, "And we'll have you for our little boy" (314). "He knew this was not true" (314) is the reported thought of the boy. Does he finally have something right, or does he once again fail to understand?

✦

"The Oedipus Complex" is one of the most successful comic stories of several decades. Its origin is surprising: Pritchett has said that it comes "straight from life. . . . It was told to me by my dentist as he was struggling with my tooth. . . . The only thing that I had to do was to write it entirely in his abrupt dialogue" (Forkner and Séjourné, 34–35). Mr. Pollfax, the dentist of the story, tells his patient he has an "Oedipus complex" because he won away from his father, a widower, the young girl his father was going to marry. But the story does not lie so much in Pollfax's personal anecdote; Pritchett's story *is* the dentist—a dentist not quite like any other. He is a "character" and a humorist himself and, more remarkably (perhaps because many dentists are a little bit like him), totally believable.

The story is virtually a comic-dramatic monologue of the nervously talkative dentist, since "Mr. P.," the narrator and the patient in the chair, gets to say (his mouth always full) only "ah" and "blah." The story has an angular and perfectly natural beginning:

> "Good morning, Mr. P.," said Mr. Pollfax, rising and drying his hands after the last patient.
> "How's Mr. P." I was always Mr. P. until I sat in the chair and he switched the lamp on and had my mouth open. Then I got a peerage.
> "That's fine, my lord," said Mr. Pollfax, having a look inside. (238)

Like many dentists, Pollfax has his set expressions, but his are funnier than most. The narrator begins to salivate heavily: "'The Great Flood begins,' said Mr. Pollfax putting a tube in my mouth and taking another weapon from the tray" (240). As a piece of the tooth on which he is working breaks off, Pollfax announces, "Mr. Pollfax in a dilemma" (241). And this is Pollfax at the most critical moment in the extraction of a fragment of a tooth: "'Don't say anything. Keep dead still. For God's sake don't let it hear you. My lords, ladies and gentlemen, pray silence for Mr. Pollfax. It's coming, it isn't. No, it isn't. It is. It is. There,' he cried, holding a fragment in his fingers" (242). The story concludes even as the dental procedure does, with Pollfax's final words, "A good and final spit, my lord and prince" (242). If Pritchett's dentist did indeed supply this piecemeal, Pritchett reveals his artistic judgment by wise selectivity, not embellishment.

✛

"Pocock Passes" is one of three stories in the volume (the other two being "It May Never Happen" and "The Sailor") about two men who have a symbiotic relationship that suddenly dissolves but leaves some revelation behind. Unlike Belton and Phillimore, seemingly bound by complementary opposed traits, the men of this story, Rogers and Pocock, appear to be doubles: both are enormously fat, both are heavy drinkers, and both, in their early fifties, having begun to "live on their capital," feel they are on the steep downslope of their lives.

At a pub Rogers, a building contractor, meets Pocock, a painter who has just come to the small village to have, he says, peace to paint. Soon the two are "drawn will-lessly together by the magnetic force of their phenomenal obesities" (226). Rogers, a married man who had nonetheless felt an aching loneliness in himself, finds his relationship with his new friend both psychologically healing and rejuvenating. He discovers in Pocock a soul mate, and "at night they [meet] like lovers" (230).

When Pocock suddenly dies, Rogers, "a jellyfish which is washed and rocked by sensations and not by thought" (224), is rocked in a way that to the reader will seem at first curious and then plausible. He must deny his spiritual brotherhood with Pocock in order to push away the frightening awareness of his own mortality. Rogers's mind is incapable of clear, sustained thought, and Pritchett's omniscient narrator offers no overt help in understanding it. But it seems Rogers needs to establish a reason that Pocock died and he did not. Perhaps, Rogers thinks, it was some kind of divine justice—Pocock, after all, painted nudes. Rogers feels ratified in this judgment by an incident that gives the story a turn toward dark comic fantasy. At a movie theater he sees a film several years old. And there, astonishingly, in one scene of the film is Pocock, a figure of fun and ridicule. He lies, as Rogers had once seen him in life, on a bed in his loud checked suit, "with a bottle, rolled on its side, near by" (236).

The story probably has no deep, analyzable meaning, but it has a curious power because of the way it deals with mystery. Rogers had taken from Pocock's possessions, as a kind of legacy, a painting of a nude, because he could not quite believe his friend would do such a painting. It "symbolized the incomprehensibility of the existence of other people" (236). And in fact Pocock remains as essentially incomprehensible to the reader as to Rogers. Should the first syllable of his name remind the reader of a British slang term for excrement, the second of male arrogance and pretentiousness? Or should the whole name be thought of as a shortened version of "Poppycock"? We can note that Pocock's reputation as a painter seems greatly exaggerated, and that apparently he did not paint at all in the village. He may be one of the many liars or deceivers in Pritchett's canon, but he sets off in his double the horrible suspicion that a joyful life is itself an imposture, that only disorder, disease, and death are real.

❖

Because plot and incident are at a bare minimum in "Many Are Disappointed," most readers will rightly suspect that the story's seemingly lightweight surface gracefully bears a heavy weight of implication. Superficially the story is about the disappointment of four young men on a rural bicycling tour when they find that the only "tavern" for miles around does not serve beer. Beneath the surface, however, its currents suggest inarticulate or half-articulate longings and desires thwarted or unrecognized.

Bert, the youngest member of the group, has romantic/erotic daydreams of meeting a young, beautiful woman at the next pub; all of the men look forward to beer, good food, and conviviality as a kind of natural reward to a morning's cycling. But the house they arrive at is, despite the TAVERN sign, no public house at all. Bert looks at "the pale-blue-veined chest of the woman" and asks incredulously, "You don't sell beer?" (261). The woman—static, submissive, and melancholic, leading a desolate life with just her little girl—briefly explains the confusion and offers, "Many are disappointed" (261). The men are forced to be content with her meal of tea, bread and butter, and tomatoes.

Pritchett's apparently trivial scene actually illuminates some partly hidden aspect of personality in the four men and the timid woman, never named, who serves them. Although it is difficult to say to what degree Pritchett was conscious of it, the story may well, as one critic suggests, "be read as a metaphor for the condition of woman, or the woman's condition,"[15] even though the story's orchestration suggests that each of the men will be visited eventually with his own disappointment. A gloomy, slightly wistful atmosphere hangs delicately in the air as Pritchett renders a kind of minimalist prose poetry that is all the more effective for its sad Chekhovian beauty and implication. The aesthetic adage that "less is often more" is here given proof.

✦

"The Sailor" and "The Saint"—the two major stories of the volume yet to be considered—are among the four or five best known of Pritchett's canon.

Pritchett has written that "the writer of short stories has to catch our attention at once not only by the novelty of his people and scene but by the distinctiveness of his voice, and to hold us by the distinctiveness of his design: for what we ask for is the sense that our now restless lives achieve shape at times and that our emotions have their architecture."[16] At about the time he wrote "The Sailor" Pritchett was quickly coming to be recognized as a writer with a distinctive voice, one that was tangy, witty, and original. Among British writers of the past 40 or 50 years he might be rivaled only by Harold Pinter in his ability to replicate in his characters' dialogue the vernacular of a certain time and place.

An identifiable Pritchettian quality exists in the opening of "The Sailor." Pritchett works on the achievement of this quality; it does not come spontaneously: "My early short story 'The Sailor' was done when I was about 30. I first wrote it in the third person, then from the god's eye viewpoint. I then discarded that draft and reworked it in the first person. Revising always improves writing."[17] The first paragraph introduces us to the sailor, probably the most memorable of all Pritchett's eccentrics:

> He was lifting his knees high and putting his hand up, when I first saw him, as if, crossing the road through that stinging rain, he were breaking through the bead curtain of a Pernambuco bar. I knew he was going to stop me. This part of the Euston Road is a beat of the men who want a cup of tea or their fare to a job in Luton or some outlying town.
>
> "Beg pardon, chum," he said in an anxious hot-potato voice. "Is that Whitechapel?" (156)

The narrator, an educated man and possibly a writer, feels sympathy for the utterly lost sailor, a man with no sense at all of direction on land. The narrator becomes thoroughly fascinated with this ex-sailor, Albert Thompson, though, when Thompson declines his offer of a drink on the grounds that "it's temptation" (157). The unnamed narrator reports, "I think it was that word which convinced me the sailor was my kind of man. I am, on the whole, glad to say that I am a puritan and the word temptation went home, painfully, pleasurably, excitingly and intimately familiar. A most stimulating and austerely gregarious word, it indicates either the irresistible hypocrite or the fellow-struggler with sin. I couldn't let him go after that" (157). The narrator invites Thompson to come to work for him at his bungalow out in the country, much in the same capacity a sailor worked for Pritchett himself in the late 1920s: "When my [first] wife was away acting in a repertory company in the north of England we found a down-and-out sailor who came down to look after me. A long time afterward, years indeed, some of these events became the basis of a story called 'The Sailor'" (*MO*, 203).

Some readers, not long into the story, may feel that it is going to be merely a whimsically cute story: Thompson's propensity for getting lost makes him seem childlike and endearing, and his naval language makes him seem lovably different: "Things were not put away; they were 'stowed.' String appeared in strange knots to make things 'fast,' plants were 'lashed' in the dying garden, washing was 'hoist' on the lines, floors were 'swabbed.' The kitchen became the 'galley.' The postman came 'alongside,' all meals were 'piped,' and at bedtime we 'piped down'" (162).

But Thompson is more than just a lovable old salt in the same sense that he is more than just an eccentric. (It is the severe human delimitation of his characters by the word *eccentric* that causes Pritchett to take issue with its application.) Admittedly, much of any reader's delight comes by way of Pritchett's effective use of two-dimensional effects of a Dickensian kind. But Pritchett gains significant thematic and aesthetic effects by strategically allowing his characters suddenly and convincingly to reveal third dimensions, reinforcing ideas emerging from the story's center about the ways in which people are guilty of undervaluing human complexity, ambiguity, and dignity in others. People also sometimes misestimate the facts: Thompson is not "just off a ship" (157), as the narrator first thinks, and the "Colonel's daughter," thought to be 25, is actually a sergeant-major's daughter, age 39. A close correspondence exists between the technique and the appearance/reality theme.

The quiet comic drama of the two puritans in conflict with certain basic needs and impulses is enacted against the backdrop of an immanently powerful, somewhat austere Nature, beautifully described:

> The bungalow where I lived was small and stood just under the brow of a hill. The country was high and stony there. The roads broke up into lanes, the lanes sunk into woods and cottages were few. The oak woods were naked

and as green as canker. They stood like old men, and below them were sweet plantations of larch where the clockwork pheasants went off like toys in the rainy afternoons. At night you heard a farm dog bark like a pistol and the oceanic sound of the trees and sometimes, over an hour and a half's walk away, the whistle of a train. But that was all. The few people looked as though they had grown out of the land, sticks and stones in cloth. . . . It was derelict country; frost with its teeth fast in the ground, the wind running finer than sand through a changeless sky or the solitary dribble of water in the butts and the rain legging it over the grass—that was all one heard or saw there. (158)

There is no self-indulgence in the simple poetic elegance of this passage (one has to go to Lawrence or a Welsh writer like Kate Roberts to find its equal). Even so, only rarely does Pritchett choose to provide brilliant, sustained descriptive passages like this in his short fiction. His unqualified assertion that "I can't write poetry to save my life" (Guppy and Weller, 194) is an extreme bit of modesty. That he almost always chooses to hold in check the poetic resources of which he is capable should cause readers to meditate on the artful qualities he has virtually pioneered and elects to use instead.

The suggestion of the narrator that he and the sailor are kindred spirits—alike in their puritanism—causes readers to form their own comparison and contrast of the two figures. As the narrator tells the reader, Thompson too has noticed the similarity between himself and his supposed benefactor: "I was like him, he said, I kept myself to myself. I kept out of temptation's way. He was glad I was like that, he said" (168). Pritchett once volunteered, "A casual overheard phrase—'I keep myself to myself'—started me writing 'Sailor.'"[18] One might suppose that this phrase is important, and in fact it is. It encourages the reader to see the two men as independent, self-reliant souls secure in their isolation, but it also suggests that they are lonely individuals afraid of human contact because it may bring the mess of emotional complication to their lives.

What fascinates the reader as the story progresses is the realization that Thompson, despite his protestations, by no means keeps himself to himself. A large token of his sociability is provided at the end of the story: as the narrator rides in a taxi to the train station along with Thompson, who is leaving to go back to London, he notes that "the police, the fishmonger, boys going to school, dozens of people waved to [Thompson]. I might have been riding with royalty" (176). Although people in the area were at first frightened of Thompson or regarded him as a mere curiosity, Thompson has managed to make significant human contact with many of them, including the Colonel's daughter, the third major character of the story. The mistress of a gas-heater salesman who has relegated her to a distant second place behind a younger mistress, the Colonel's daughter seems a somewhat shabby, somewhat vulgar version of an archetypal temptress living in a ruined, weed-crowded Eden. The narrator has fixed her as "the hardest drinking and most blasphemous piece of apparent childish innocence you had ever seen" (160). She is, though, a full human being with her own separate identity—a lively, quick-witted, lonely woman whose innate disposition prevents her from masochistically enjoying the ache of loneliness. Her overtures to the narrator have been rejected, but those to the sailor almost surely have not. They are two people with a need for other people, and this aspect makes them more fortunate than the narrator. She and Thompson return to the narrator's bungalow late one night, both of them happily drunk. The sailor's eyes have "a look of wild love of all the world" (173); "her eyes [are] warm and shining," and "she pick[s] leaves off her skirt," which is "undone" (174). The whole next day Thompson behaves as if all is perfectly normal, and it certainly appears that he is only, at the prompting of the narrator, paying lip service to their common puritanism when he mechanically reprehends, toward evening, the events of the previous night.

The very essence of "The Sailor" is its wry comedy; although the theme of moral revelation is present at the story's center, the narrative steers the reader toward it only in zigzag fashion. Pritchett's readers do not need to be informed that appearances are often deceptive, but it is the small, sometimes intricate differences between both appearance and reality and order and disorder that feed the more subtle comedy in the story and move forward its serious theme.

Thompson exemplifies certain ambivalences common to everyone because they are part of human nature. He has obviously felt the effects of disorder in his own life. He is lonely and nervous; it seems that he has been invalided out of the navy because of his ulcers. His propensity for getting hopelessly lost is so genuine and so severe that we would term it today a learning disability. The ex-sailor, though, creates his own breakwaters against the threatening waves of disorder. He is a meticulous housekeeper who soon has the narrator's home shipshape. While consciously he thinks that the avoidance of temptation will provide him with a barrier of security, his instinctual wisdom tells him that isolation from others is not going to sustain him spiritually in this life. As the narrator says of Thompson, when he goes out he almost always follows people "to their doorsteps, drifting to their allotments, backyards, and, all the time, telling them, as he clung to their company, about the dangers of human intercourse. 'I never speak to nobody'—it was untrue, but it was not a lie. It was simply a delusion" (168). The sailor, like everyone in life, goes on searching (he is again seeking Whitechapel—the name of this real London district nicely suggesting a knightly quest—at the end of the story), but his gift, even if he does not realize it, for human connectedness sustains him on his way.

It is partly true but also somewhat facile to maintain that the narrator, because of his divorcement from people and his tendency to see them as characters or types, is emotionally or spiritually sterile. He admits that he may be a prig—"[the Colonel's daughter] was right, I was a prig" (171). Some readers tend to see him also as a repressed homosexual, but the story does not provide sufficient support for that opinion. When the Colonel's daughter says, presumably in a joshing way, "I see you got the Navy down here. I didn't know you were that way,", the narrator comfortably and quickly goes along with her joke and replies, "I thought you would have guessed that straight away" (161). The narrator is a man of judgment, wit, and sensibility, but even a man such as this will sometimes not know himself. The Colonel's daughter accuses him of naïveté: "Oh, you know a hell of a lot, don't you? I don't say you're not an interesting man, but you don't get on with it, do you?" (169).

Whether the narrator consciously convicts himself of living a spiritually desolate life is problematic. One of the most lyrical passages in the story—and with Pritchett we must assume that such passages are functionally important—suggests that a realization of this sort is rising to the narrator's level of consciousness. It is the night that Thompson goes out, the night that he is to end in the arms of the Colonel's daughter, and the narrator is thinking about how Thompson has yielded to temptation:

> I was disappointed in Thompson. Really, not to have had more guts than that! Restlessly, I looked out of the window. There was a full moon spinning on the tail of a dying wind. Under the moonlight the fields were like wideawake faces, the woods like womanish heads of hair upon them. I put on my hat and coat and went out. I was astonished by the circle of stars. They were as distinct as figures on a clock. I took out my watch and compared the small time in my hand with the wide time above. Then I walked on. There was a sour smell at the end of the wood, where, no doubt, a dead rabbit or pigeon was rotting. (172)

In the narrator's fancy, one perhaps born of thwarted desire and self-accusation, the fields are awake at night and seem to lie in the embrace of the womanly woods, a female moon is moved by a masculine wind, and the stars, although distinct, are not alone—they are eternally united with one another in a circle of perfection. Nothing is cut off and alone like the narrator except for the dead and rotting pigeon or rabbit between his house and the wood. Pritchett, always preferring extreme subtlety in his best stories, gives no clear signal that the narrator achieves an epiphany at this or any other point. Shucking off puritanism is more than a conscious recognition followed by a simple act of will. Pritchett refuses to sacrifice the complex and even paradoxical truths of the world, or the contingent nature of events, for the sake of a neat ending. Whether Thompson and the narrator turn out to be more foils than doubles is a question that can be argued vigorously on either side. Some readers will find the theme unresolved; others will find it nicely understated.

✦

"The Saint" is a satiric arrow directed at a religion much like Christian Science (in which Pritchett himself had been raised), but it is also more than that. It is both an initiation story and a comic story of pith, wit, and character. It has an angular, arresting beginning: "When I was seventeen years old I lost my religious faith" (187).

We learn that the narrator and his family have recently been converted to the "sect called the Church of the Last Purification, of Toronto, Canada" (187). The sect's chief article of belief is that evil is but an illusion; "error" is belief in evil: "We regarded it as 'Error'—our name for Evil—to believe the evidence of our senses, and if we had influenza or consumption, or had lost our money or were unemployed, we denied the reality of these things, saying that since God could not have made them they therefore did not exist" (187).

The young man has powerful religious doubts and is thus the intended recipient of a heart-to-heart talk from Hubert Timberlake, an esteemed and avuncular leader of the sect. Timberlake is the butt of Pritchett's satiric humor, but despite "his torpid enamelled smile" (189) he is not a caricature. He is not such a pompous fuddy-duddy that he cannot react with intelligence and wit to what is going on around him: When Timberlake arrives the narrator's uncle, a "humorous man," says to him of his nephew, "He thinks he thinks, Mr. Timberlake, but I tell him he only thinks he does" (189). Timberlake knows how to win over the young man: he instantaneously replies, "What say we tell your uncle it's funny he thinks he's funny" (190). This chief "Purifier" enjoys success until he decides that the important talk with the young doubter might best be held while they engage in the young man's favorite activity, punting on the river. Timberlake insists on doing the punting, calmly proclaiming past skill in the art. "How's that, you guys?" (193) is his self-congratulatory question as he successfully pushes off. But not sufficiently heedful of the boy's warning to watch out for the low-hanging branches of a willow tree, Timberlake is soon in danger of falling into the river. He grasps at the branch that hit him; then, as it sags beneath his weight, grasps at a higher one until he is suspended for a time a foot or so above the river as the punt proceeds downstream. (The tableau of the religious dignitary's clutching the sagging branch is probably the most memorably humorous in all of Pritchett's fiction.) It suddenly enters the boy's mind that he might have to endure the psychological shock and upset of a miracle: "I prayed with all my might that Mr. Timberlake would not walk upon the water" (195). The doubt is resolved momentarily: "It was my prayer and not his that was answered" (195).

The boy sees Timberlake's shoes dip into the river, and then sees the water rise above Timberlake's ankles and up his socks. Timberlake stretches to try for a grip on a still higher branch, and as he does so his coat and waistcoat rise and part from his trousers. To the boy it is "like a fatal flaw in a statue, an earthquake crack which [makes] the monumental mortal. . . It was at this moment I realized the final revelation about man and society had come to nobody and that Mr. Timberlake knew nothing at all about the origin of evil" (195). But if Timberlake knows nothing about the origin of evil, his efforts to live up to being a saint are almost Herculean. If he refuses to recognize humiliation, then no humiliation has occurred; the narrator tells us that Timberlake took "the line that nothing had happened" (196). As Timberlake sits in the sun and watches steam rise from his clothes, the narrator is sure that the "stoutish," out-of-shape Saint is telling himself he is not wet. Readers will be torn between delight at the hilariously appropriate exposure of all Timberlake represents and sympathetic admiration for a stoicism that is amazingly well maintained under conditions that are most trying because most ridiculous. But the ridiculous reaches its zenith when Timberlake, rising from the riverbank where, fully clothed, he had been lying, reveals that his wet black suit is now altogether covered with buttercup pollen. Timberlake sees this but only raises "his thin eyebrows a little," causing the narrator to feel that "the man's a saint. . . . As saintly as any of those gold-leaf figures in the churches of Sicily" (198).

The narrator tells the story 16 years after Timberlake's unwilling immersion in the river. He has been reflecting vividly on that day because he has just heard news of Timberlake's death. Nonmeticulous readers will be somewhat puzzled by the ending: "I understood why he did not talk to me [that fateful day 16 years earlier] about the origin of evil. He was honest. The ape was with us. The ape that merely followed me was already inside Mr. Timberlake eating out his heart" (199). The "ape" is identified for the reader toward the beginning of the story as an abiding religious doubt that springs from a contemplation of evil in the world: "Without warning and as if I had gone into my bedroom at night and had found a gross ape seated in my bed and thereafter following me about with his grunts and his fleas and a look, relentless and ancient scored on his brown face. I was faced with the problem which prowls at the centre of all religious faith. I was faced by the difficulty of the origin of evil" (188).

Timberlake was a man temperamentally disposed to giving the very center of his being to his religion. When the ape of doubt had destroyed that center, nothing was left to the man except a memory and a pretense. As Timberlake had sat sodden and golden in his clothes that day long past, the boy had suddenly had the correct intuition that Timberlake "was a dull man, duller than any man I have ever known" (197). The narrator grew out of childhood into adulthood that day, but other people—such as adherents of the strange sect—cling childishly to simple illusions. The real world is complex and threatening, but those who try to hide themselves from it do so at great peril to themselves. The price of self-deception is usually high; in "The Sailor" and "The Saint" characters are victimized by deceptions that become institutionalized in religious sects or traditions whose base is flawed or far too narrow.

The Sailor, Sense of Humour, and Other Stories

In the 1950s the publication history of Pritchett stories in book form became more complex. The volume to appear after *It May Never Happen* was *Collected Stories*, published by Chatto & Windus in London in 1956. It contains all the stories of *You Make Your Own Life* and *It May Never Happen* and nine other stories previously uncollected ("The Sniff," "The Collection," "The Satisfactory," "The Ladder," "Passing the Ball," "Things as They Are," "The Landlord," "A Story of Don Juan," and "Double Divan") for a total of 37 stories. A new American collection, *The Sailor, Sense of Humour, and Other Stories,* was published by Knopf in 1956; it contains seven stories from *You Make Your Own Life,* 13 from *It May Never Happen,* and five not previously collected ("The Sniff," "The Satisfactory," "Passing the Ball,"

"Things as They Are," and "The Landlord"), for a total of 25 stories.

✤

"The Satisfactory" is a droll story of psychological exposure set against the backdrop of World War II air raids and food shortages. Plymbell, an antiques dealer and decorator, is inclined to see the war as "essentially an attack on gastronomy, on the stomach and palate of the human race" (364). Each day at luncheon he scowls at a restaurant's "farcical menu" (365) but is partly consoled by the food his shabby and thin secretary, Miss Tell, surreptitiously slips across the table to him. When Miss Tell's mother and father are killed in an air raid and Plymbell learns that she has her parents' ration books as well as her own, his hunger and avarice further increase. Miss Tell is hungry not for food but for a sustaining love relationship; she has been hurt by thrice being "the other woman" (378). (Like Janey of "The Ladder," she can think about nothing except prostrating herself before her boss.) Wry, delicate dramatic ironies are present throughout the story. Readers will think they understand—and they probably will understand rightly—that which Miss Tell seems not to notice: Plymbell is self-absorbed, vain, and a probable homosexual. The trade of food for love would not in any case seem promising; in the case of Plymbell it would seem far from satisfactory. But in wartime everything is sped up and magnified—the cravings of neither Plymbell nor Miss Tell should be underestimated. Strange things happen in wartime, and the drollery of the ending in no way clashes with probability: "The satisfactory had occurred" (380).

✤

"Passing the Ball" provides a droll commentary on the bored, petty lives of the people of an upper-middle-class county set. The tone is one of compassion and amusement rather than anger, seeming to suggest that some people's stratagems for filling emptiness are probably not very much inferior to other people's.

✤

"The Landlord" gives readers a psychological glimpse into the grim realities of a difficult marriage by filtering it through the dual lenses of comedy and fantasy of a slightly Jamesian sort. The wife, who is self-important, aggressive, and a relentless social climber, has totally submerged her husband, who dares do nothing but what she wishes. At her insistence they buy a semidetached house in a posh neighborhood; the man who sells it to them lives next door. Strangely, the man still acts as if he owns their house; he lets himself in with a key, takes baths, sits down to meals, and eventually begins to sleep in the bedroom. The wife, Mrs. Seugar, is flattered to be on such close terms with someone of the upper crust and thus chooses to say nothing. The henpecked Mr. Seugar, like someone in a dream, feels impotent indignation at the liberties of the "landlord." One day the landlord stops Mr. Seugar on the stairs and says peremptorily that he is looking for *his* wife when it is obvious he means Mrs. Seugar. This sets up the humorous punch ending of the story. The husband suddenly recognizes that fate, perhaps in the form of mental disease in the landlord, has presented him with the chance of a lifetime: he moves by himself into the landlord's house. The story succeeds in a way that all good psychological fantasies do: the strange events are made to have an uncanny plausibility.

✦

Like many of Pritchett's stories, "The Ladder" presents a situation wherein buried emotional truths are suddenly unearthed. The 15-year-old narrator is visiting her father for summer vacation. Her parents have recently divorced, and the father has already married Janey, his secretary of 15 years. The weight of the too-familiar, projected on him by both his past and present wives, creates greater psychological burdens for the man than he consciously recognizes. In some ways the boundaries between the two women have become blurred in his mind (an echo of the blurred boundaries motif in the fantastical "The Landlord"). His first wife had always wanted the house remodeled and he had always refused; his second wife does not want the house changed and he *is* having it remodeled. His decision to renovate is intended as a taunt to the first wife, but it also annoys his present wife, something he perhaps subconsciously intends. Janey is greatly put out by the necessity—entailed by the renovation—of having to use a ladder to get to the second floor (emblematic of shaky, impermanent connections of all sorts). She also feels the strain of having to be nice to her new stepdaughter; the two do not get along.

As the 15-year-old and her father go out one day, the girl willfully removes the ladder, stranding Janey in the upstairs of the house for six hours. When they return Janey is red-faced and very upset, but the father and daughter soon join each other in laughing. The daughter apologizes three days later; Janey, however, leaves for good shortly thereafter. The girl's father realizes he has made a mistake.

The father in the story is one of the large number of Pritchett's characters who are self-deceived. Although the story is a bit too thin to be one of Pritchett's very best, it has, as the best do, a sense of easiness and noncontrivance accompanied by a great weight of thematic implication and subtle artistry. The handling of internal conflicts (need for permanence/need for change, domination/submission, retribution/genuine self-fulfillment) is effectively understated.

Assured and Unhurried Artistry

Between the mid-1940s and the 1961 publication of *When My Girl Comes Home*, Pritchett had devoted most of his energies to editorial work for the *New Statesman*, various kinds of nonfiction, especially criticism, and the novel *Mr. Beluncle* (1951). Although more than most professional writers Pritchett was still able to publish his short stories, he did have some trouble with rejections and, like many writers, was probably depressed by both the declining market for short stories and the low rates of payment offered by magazines. In 1966 he referred to the short story as "one of the inextinguishable lost causes"[19] and noted that "the economics of short-story writing are grim but eccentric. For twenty-five years I myself was paid ludicrous sums for all my stories: three pounds for 'The Sailor,' working up to ten pounds. All my stories were rejected by the magazines that paid respectably in England and America" ("TSS," 8).

When My Girl Comes Home

When My Girl Comes Home shows a slight falling off from the excellence of *It May Never Happen*, several of the stories being slight and inclined toward trick endings. The stories continue to be punctuated with wryly comic ironies; however, because those ironies are predicated on readers' apprehension of the nuances of class distinction, the stories will have a more limited appeal for many Americans.

✦

Pritchett has maintained that "When My Girl Comes Home" is the best story he has ever written,"[20] but some readers are prepared to argue the point, feeling that it is one of the stories in which Pritchett goes too far with the technique of implicitness. Under a review headed "The Temptations of a Technique" an anonymous *Times Literary Supplement* reviewer opined that "one may perhaps feel that its obliquities and lacunae are as much the result of the temptations of a teasing technique as of artistic necessity."[21]

The novella-length (about 20,000 words) "When My Girl Comes Home," with its extremely subtle, indirect approach to its thematic ideas and with its large cast of characters (10 major ones), places heavy demands on the reader. Pritchett says he was aware of this factor when he wrote the story: "It's my favourite because so many people have said that you couldn't write a short story about a large number of people, and—just taking a bet—I thought it must be possible. It's awfully difficult to connect the people and events in a way that is natural, without intervening to tell the reader what is happening, and I found a way by luck. The rather Meredithian notion of people reporting to each other suddenly came to me, and I managed to prevent myself from closing the story" (Haffenden, 228).

The story takes place in the immediate postwar years, a time when ordinary citizens of the warring nations were trying to establish a psychological equilibrium, to separate fact from rumor, and to assure themselves that they had steady footholds in a moral world. The "teasing technique" is employed not for its own sake but because it effectively conveys the theme, projecting the reader into a 1940s world of moral and epistemological uncertainty.

The story is set in the fictional Hincham Street, a relatively closed, small, suburban-type community within London, insular and insulated, like many such places, until the forces of twentieth-century history blew cracks in its foundation. Hincham Street seemed to totter and shift, causing the familiar to fall against the alien and increasing the feeling of disequilibrium. As the story begins it is difficult to distinguish the apparent from the real, good from evil. To judge is perhaps to be morally smug and self-righteous; not to attempt to discriminate at all is to give way to slackness and cause the erosion of one's moral nature. The story, while irreducible to any easily paraphrasable meaning, has suggestions about it of being a parable for its time. If it is a somewhat puzzling parable, that is probably because the times are puzzling.

All who have commented on the story in print have seen the initial irony: the Hilda who arrives home on Hincham Street is not the one her family and neighbors expect. They await the arrival of a pitiable, near-broken, and perhaps half-starved figure, triumphant with the joy of release or eager to be held in the comforting embrace of Hincham Street. They are all taken aback but happy when an unperturbed, indeed rather placid Hilda returns, looking healthy and prosperous and trailing a dozen pieces of cream-colored luggage containing six evening dresses and other expensive personal effects. The appearance/reality theme is underlined when we learn that Hilda was not a POW in a Japanese camp but the wife of a Japanese soldier.

But a further set of ironies involving Hilda Johnson and illusion/reality has been generally neglected. With the surprise of her prosperity and with the thrill of seeing her story in the newspapers, the neighbors regard Hilda as a larger-than-life figure, a major case for consideration. The neighbors do what the young narrator, Harry Fraser, does, and what the reader too is compelled to do: subject Hilda to scrutiny, questions, hypotheses, suppositions, judgments. Is Hilda a wily deceiver? Is she a person living in a world of self-constructed illusion? (Are there really two American suitors?) Is she a selfish, pampered, overage girl? Is she morally and intellectually vacuous? ("To young Mrs. Draper Hilda seemed a 'bit simple'" [479].) Does she lead an unprincipled sex life? (Constance calls her a whore [478].)

The irony resides in the fact that her family and neighbors begin to treat Hilda as a character in a novel, not as a real person. She neither deserves nor can comfortably bear dramatically intense scrutiny. Her neighbors reduce her humanity and that of her mother (who physically dies); they metaphorically steal part of her; and one of them, Bill Williams, literally steals nearly all her possessions. The irony is extended by our being encouraged by the narrator and the other people of Hincham Street to think that surely there is much more to Hilda than meets the eye. But is there? Unlike most major characters in literature, she may be exactly what she seems and what she says she is. The literature/life opposition seems to be invoked as well as that of appearance/reality. The story's evidence suggests that the war at first numbed the mind but, toward its conclusion, overcharged the imagination (468–69).

Hilda, taking things as they come, seems ultimately a quite ordinary individual—she is not guileful, conceited, selfish, or lazy. She is mostly trusting and a bit obtuse. A less innocent woman would have arrived without the smart luggage and would somehow have concealed the other luxury items. Hilda seems not particularly spoiled or pampered: she is content to sleep in a small bed in a small room with her old mother, and she does more than her fair share of the household chores. The neighbors simply have a hugely overinflated image of Hilda. Harry Fraser comes close to recognizing Hincham Street's enlarged vision of Hilda, significantly speaking of "dream," "visions," and "fancies" and referring to the cinema (where an evening's entertainment entwined romance, horror, and newsreel to complex psychological and aesthetic effects): "We had been disturbed in a very long dream. We had been living on inner visions for years. It was an effect of the long war. England had been a prison. Even the sky was closed, and, like convicts, we had been driven to dwelling on fancies in our dreary minds. In the cinema the camera sucks some person forward into an enormous close-up and holds a face there yards wide, filling the whole screen, all holes and pores, like some sucking octopus that might eat up an audience many rows at a time" (454).

Pritchett's successful strategy is to make his reader so much one with the people who have placed Hilda under a mercilessly bright lamp that we fail to see that they are involved in a morally distorted pursuit. In their natural desire to pin things down they fail to apprehend sufficiently the randomness and fluidity of life that Pritchett softly but continuously seems to insist on in his fiction. The last word of the story is *us*—"[The American friend's book] was about us" (491). That should tell readers, who should not exclude themselves from the *us*, that the story is not nearly so much about a quite ordinary Hilda Johnson as it is about our habits of flawed perception, our simplistic moralities, for we as readers have been doing the very same thing as the people of the London suburb.

"When My Girl Comes Home" is built on a pattern found in many of Pritchett's stories but is here extended. It is, as we have seen in "The Sailor" and "Pocock Passes," that of a protagonist, narrator, or central consciousness superficially living a stable, contented life. A figure from outside, usually flamboyant or of dubious respectability, arrives on the scene. The outsider strikes some deeply responsive chords in the protagonist and a symbiotic relationship is established. After a time, however, either something shocking happens to the outsider or something disconcerting is revealed about him, causing the protagonist to come to some disturbing awareness about himself, whether he wishes to recognize it or not. In this, the most complex of all Pritchett's stories, the protagonist is "Hincham Street"—Harry Fraser, the narrator, thematically standing in for all his neighbors. Hilda, the "girl who returns to them from afar," catalyzes many emotions in the collective protagonist, bringing these people of Hincham Street close to self-revelation.

✦

A simpler but related pattern is found in "The Wheelbarrow." The most common pattern in Pritchett's stories, it presents two people briefly coming together and setting off a spark or two, and then moving apart. Unlike the previous pattern, this one will not draw a protagonist and an outsider as alter egos; nor will it conclude with the protagonist's experiencing any self-revelation.

The story is successful partly because it transcends the materials Pritchett first seems to provide. Susan Lohafer vividly describes the plot readers may think they see developing: "A Welsh miner [turned cabby and preacher] is admitted to the garden, house, and family secrets of an unattached, school-teachery but rousable woman—well you have almost a parody of the sort of a story that brings a match to the wood. The outmoded rubbage, conveyed in the strident wheelbarrow, pushed by the virile Robert, does indeed end up on a literal pyre. But does our heroine burn in flames à la Lawrence?"[22] The answer, of course, is no. Pritchett is writing a comic-ironic drama of character, and he plays almost parodically with conventions of plot and character.

Readers may also be miscued into seeing Robert Evans as a purely satiric figure—a stereotype Pritchett uses to take a satiric swipe at the Welsh. Robert is very much like the figures in the fiction of another Evans, Caradoc Evans (1883–1945), a Welsh satirist who indignantly insisted that "cant and hypocrisy and chapel belong to Wales, and no one writing about Wales can dodge them."[23] Caradoc Evans frequently provides heavy satiric portraiture of Nonconformist chapels, self-righteous congregations, immoral and hypocritical preachers and deacons, secret lusts, and supposedly pious people who worship their real gods, money and earthly goods.

Robert Evans is wily, brash, and hypocritical, but he is also amusing, genuinely appealing, and very human in his faults. He is no straw-man figure of hypocrisy; if he were, he would not exert the fascination that he does on Miss Freshwater's niece, a woman who is not naive. Their verbal and psychological duels are genuine but also good-natured and playful. Their badinage is easy and familiar, and they are not afraid of revealing themselves to each other, for their expectation is that they will never see each other again after the next few days. She taunts him by quoting biblical passages; he comments scornfully on the wasteful expense of a dress now moth-eaten, and she quotes mockingly, "Where moth and dust doth corrupt" (414). As they consider what to discard, she, "as a dig of malice at him," talks about what should be "saved" and what should be "cast into the flames" (414). They speak to each other banteringly across the great British divide of class, and the sequence of their meetings provides "a subtle play of shifting dominance—in the areas of social status, moral leverage, conversational wit, and sexual teasing" (Lohafer, 150). But at times their conversation becomes serious. Miss Freshwater's niece feels deep pangs of nostalgia and the onset of melancholia as she goes through family treasures and mementos of her own past.

After noticing her weakness, Evans, probably with mixed motives, compels her to talk about her failed marriage, her divorce, and the subsequent death of her ex-husband. He tells her how he was converted while trapped in a mineshaft during a cave-in. He shows perceptivity and sensitivity when he tells her that he could see, as she looked with emotion at some old photographs, that she was down "the dark mine of the past" (423). It is at this point that she stops mocking him.

Once the serious identifying bond between the two is established, the relationship loses much of its joshing nature. But it cannot be elevated to any higher plane. Although Evans is sexually and perhaps even amorously attracted to her, she is not likewise disposed. When he makes advances toward her, she knows exactly how to put him off. She has correctly sensed that his secret lust for the wheelbarrow is stronger than his lust for her, and she suggests that he take it. He agrees, saying, "Thank you, ma'am" (425). She realizes that the small drama between the two of them is now over: "It was the first time he had called her ma'am. The word was like a blow. The affair was over. It was, she realized, a dismissal" (425). She can consciously recognize, though, that his attitude provided some needed reassurance as to her sexual attractiveness. She thinks to herself, "He got what he wanted! And I'm evidently not as old as I look," and a moment later she concludes, "I owe Evans a lot" (426).

Pritchett's portrait of Miss Freshwater's niece is adept, all the coloration of class and background being painted in with exactitude. But it is Evans who captivates the reader's attention even as he captivates his employer. He is both genuinely charming and hypocritical. Furthermore, we do not expect his kind of sensitivity and discernment in the typical rogue. The end of the story provides exactly the right finishing touch to his portrait: he outrageously converts his experience with Miss Freshwater's niece into a kind of parable as he "witnesses" to his congregation in the field. His voice booms through a loudspeaker, "I was a slave of the strange woman the Bible tells about, the whore of Babylon, in her palace where moth and dust . . . [Pritchett's ellipsis] and burned the adulteress in the everlasting fire, my friends, and all her property" (427–28).

✦

"The Fall" also blends comedy, revelation of character, and class consciousness. Charles Peacock, an accountant at an annual accountants' dinner, amazes his peers by his expert demonstration of a stage fall. Peacock's audience is amused at first, but when Peacock almost compulsively repeats his pratfall time after time, they become bored. Readers are allowed to piece together the clues that explain the bizarre behavior of a respected man in a traditionally staid profession. His colleagues do not suspect it, but Peacock is painfully insecure: "No one who saw Peacock in his office, in Board Rooms, on committees, at meetings, knew the exhausting number of rough sketches that had to be made before the naked Peacock could become Peacock dressed for his part" (430). Two causes of this insecurity rise closer to the surface the more Peacock drinks at the dinner: his extreme sensitivity and defensiveness about his parents' having owned a fried-fish shop and his jealousy of his brother, Shelmerdine Peacock, a famous stage and film actor. Deserted by his real audience and thoroughly drunk, he performs before an imaginary one and, on concluding, falls flat on his face because he never learned to bow properly. On one level the constant falls are simply a desperate plea for attention; on another level they symbolize how Peacock's feelings of unworthiness unconsciously produce a desire for self-punishment, somewhat like that of Tom Coram in "Handsome Is as Handsome Does." "Dressed for his part," the man tries to strut like a peacock, but within he feels naked and insignificant.

The Key to My Heart

Of the stories that appear in *When My Girl Comes Home* the only significant one not yet mentioned is the last, "The Key to My Heart." Apparently Pritchett had, with good reason, become enamored of his character creations in that story, and decided to prolong their life. He used the same characters for two other stories, "Noisy Flushes the Birds" and "Noisy in the Doghouse," these additional two appearing, as did the original, first in the *New Yorker*. In 1964 Pritchett published the three stories together in book form under the title *The Key to My Heart*, with the subtitle "A Comedy in Three Parts." Not unsensibly, the Random House dust jacket refers to the book as a novel, the three stories being tightly, integrally, and progressively linked together. Because it is a book of about 37,000 words, we can remark on only a few of its features.

The novel is an immensely entertaining, very English social comedy whose droll humor is all the more delicious for its accuracy, particularly the successful way it captures small-town English life. The two main characters, Noisy Brackett and his wife, Sally, belong to the county gentry and are nothing if not eccentric. Readers who know that unofficial but longstanding British tradition tolerates and often expects eccentricity will more appreciate these very believable characters. For readers not aware of the English fondness for oddity, Pritchett has smoothly inserted a character—Mrs. Fraser, the narrator's mother, who runs a bakery with him—to provide testimony to the worshipfully high regard in which local aristocrats, particularly the more eccentric ones, can be held. Bob tells us that "Dad and Mother never minded being owed by the rich. They had both grown up in the days when you were afraid of offending people, and to hear my mother talk you would have thought that by asking the well-off to fork out you were going to kill the goose that lays the golden egg, knock the bottom out of society, and let a Labour government in" (563).

It is sometimes said that only Britons can fully appreciate a writer like Pritchett because only Britons will be alive to the subtle nuances of class and status that preoccupy the characters of both socially realistic and satiric fiction. There is truth to this, yet an opposed contention may be convincing too: that "very English" writers—Evelyn Waugh, P. G. Wodehouse, Sylvia Townsend Warner, V. S. Pritchett, Angus Wilson, and many more—appeal to the kind of American Anglophile who is predisposed toward finding most things English (or at least southern English) endearing for their qualities of either good taste or idiosyncrasy. These authors' American success (in which the *New Yorker* played a fair part) must make us seriously consider the point. Reacquaintance with ingredients already familiar to the comic taste buds makes them all the more delicious; consider, for example, Pritchett's choice of a name and residence—Major Dingle of the Old Rectory. Or that Bob Fraser's mother should bathe in the glow that she has been conditioned to think emanates from the local aristocracy, much in the same way that the doings of the Royal Family can provide the nutriment of fascination to the lives of otherwise starved people. And yet, of course, the writers mentioned do not manufacture their characters and attitudes out of whole cloth. Pritchett has humorously exaggerated, but he has, stylishly and entertainingly, captured truth.

Detractors may say that certain Americans—exemplified perhaps by the *New Yorker*—have for too long encouraged us to admire fiction depicting the English as delightfully quaint, and urge that we get over our fascination with the outmoded social manners of an insular people forming a minute part of the population of a fast-changing world. Defenders of *The Key to My Heart* must admit that it is purely escapist entertainment, though of a superior kind.

Extending his range and aiming here at pure entertainment, Pritchett allows his story to be far more plot-driven than usual and even uses farce effectively. He does so while showing no sign of strain; in fact, his narrative style—light, assured, and unselfconscious—will remind many readers of the classically light and easy touch of Evelyn Waugh. Pritchett has said,

> I suppose I've been guilty of exposing characters just because they're amusing, but I think I've usually gone beyond that. I wrote a group of stories [*The Key to My Heart*] about an air pilot called Noisy, for example, which are

farcical stories, because I am a great admirer of Chekhov who could write any kind of story. I think a writer ought to be able to write any kind of story, and therefore I don't regard myself as having any moral obligations to it. Farce is very often tragedy out of uniform. It's difficult to write, and it goes at a certain speed. . . . I am always trying to think of a bolder or more dangerous idea. (Haffenden, 224–25)

Blind Love and Other Stories

Symptomatic of the difficulties with magazine publication continuing to face Pritchett and other British short-story writers in the 1960s is that, of the 10 stories collected in *Blind Love and Other Stories* (1969), only one, "The Cage Birds," had been previously published in Britain, and that in a magazine *(Queen)* not especially known for high-quality fiction. Pritchett was by now relying even more heavily on the *New Yorker*, which had published four of these stories: "Debt of Honor," "The Liars," "The Nest Builder," and "The Skeleton." Another story, "The Speech," appeared in *Harper's*. "Blind Love," at about 17,500 words, is novella length, too long for publication in the great majority of periodicals, and the other three stories are of somewhat dubious merit. But Pritchett was probably concerned about not being able to have his stories published consistently in his own country, at least not by periodicals able to provide anything like fair compensation. A certain tidiness, a certain slickness, and an uncharacteristic push toward epiphanic moments is clearly detectable in some of the stories in *Blind Love*, and one naturally wonders if Pritchett was thinking about where he could place his stories.

The stories of *Blind Love* are all comedies, but the best are a combination of the wry, the witty, the ironic, and the deceptively subtle. All the stories are about love, if we understand that love can be thwarted, unrecognized, dammed up, or misdirected. "Blind love" can mean blind because of love, blind to one's own love or that of someone else, or a blind, unreserved plunge into love. Love is the great human catalyst, capable of effectuating the most surprising changes, even if only in the ways people see themselves. Hidden selves lurk beneath surface selves, and love often bids these hidden selves to come blindly forth. Pritchett, in short, plays interesting changes on the themes of love and blindness. While Pritchett probably issued himself no instruction about writing stories around a certain theme, it would seem he thought about the theme of difficulties associated with love as he made his selection for *Blind Love*.

✦

"Blind Love" has several kinds of complexity. It is different, however, from most of Pritchett's other very best stories (an exception being "Handsome Is as Handsome Does," which it does resemble), in that he works out, relatively explicitly, hidden emotions and motives of the sort he would usually leave to his readers' imaginations. But even if Pritchett does in a somewhat old-fashioned sense explicitly lay open the "psychology" of his characters, the story is far subtler and richer than it might at first appear. True, the basic situation is diagrammatically neat: a well-to-do lawyer, totally blind, was deserted by his wife some 20 years before, when he began to go blind. His present secretary-companion, a woman now 39, was abandoned years before by her husband when he discovered, only after their marriage, that she had a birthmark extending from her neck to below one breast. At the end of the story the blind employer, undeterred by a physical blemish he now knows about but cannot see, comes together with his secretary to form a mutual relationship of love, sexual fulfillment, and understanding.

A bare-bones summary like this so simplifies and distorts the story that it deprives it of meaning. What each of the two main characters—who are given almost equal emphasis—thinks, feels, fears, hopes, and desires says, of course, much about the general human condition and human possibility. But the story is successful precisely because the characters' physical defects are not just bold metaphors for spiritual defects or sempiternal human weakness and limitation. Both Armitage, the blind lawyer, and Mrs. Johnson, his secretary and general factotum, are unique persons and highly individuated characters; their believability issues from their distinct personalities and complex, even contradictory impulses. They are not characters out of a soap opera, but they are not the pale figures of allegory either.

Quite naturally, Armitage and Mrs. Johnson are both afraid of exposure and humiliation. Armitage, professionally successful, is always dignified and proud but is particularly sensitive and stubborn about his ability to get around his house on his own. It would probably hurt him worse to have someone pity him than despise him. His capable self-reliance truly impresses everyone, but we soon wonder, as Mrs. Johnson comes to do, what strenuous preparations, what tediously repeated acts of will the poor man must perform in private so that he will not "humiliate" himself before someone else. In attempting to overcome his handicap, maintain self-respect, and not shut himself off from a "full" life, he has erected a barrier between the inner and outer self and has thus cut himself off to a degree he does not consciously admit to himself. Pritchett, of course, gives no signal that his readers should feel wiser or more knowing than Armitage; the author is tolerant and understanding in his sympathies.

Helen Johnson also lives a double life. On the surface she is consistent, virtuous, and practical; a "cheery soul" (632) and a realistic Cockney with a frank face; a confident woman who dares say what she thinks. She seems free of neurosis, and one would suspect she is mostly what she seems. Her mask is a good one, but she too is torn inside. She sees herself "as a punished and self-hating person [who] was drawn to work with a punished man" (639). Her outer cheerfulness belies the inner self-hatred, and her apparent habits of effortless virtue mask the "creature [that] craved for the furtive, for the hand that slipped under a skirt, for the scuffle in the back seat of a car, for a five-minute disappearance into a locked office" (643). She tells Armitage she has had no other lover besides her husband, but in actuality she has had "three or four" (648). Mrs. Johnson's "ineradicable bloody insult" (637) has long impelled her to the habit of concealment, but this habit exacts a heavy toll because it creates a cleft in the self. Love and deception have long been confusedly intertwined in Mrs. Johnson. She thinks back to the period of courtship with her husband, and about why she could not bring herself to tell him about the birthmark: "How could she have been such a fool as to deceive her husband? It was not through wickedness. She had been blinded too—blinded by love; in a way love had made her so full of herself that, perhaps, she had never seen *him*. And her deceptions: she could not stop herself smiling at them, but they were really pitiable because she was so afraid of losing him and to lose him would be to lose this now beautifully deluded self" (637).

In some ways Mrs. Johnson's physical impairment causes her more suffering than Armitage's does him. Her impairment has been successfully concealed for many years in ordinary life, but the secrecy itself causes deep uneasiness. She carries too the psychologically damaging equation of the birthmark with lost love, or love never won. She senses that exposure of her shame, rather than continued concealment, might help ease the psychological burden, and that may be one of the reasons she nude-sunbathes the time she happens to be seen by Mr. Smith, the bogus faith healer. While in a highly emotional state she confesses to Armitage that the "Peeping Jesus . . . saw the lot" and that "You can't see it, you silly fool. The whole bloody Hebrides, the whole plate of liver" (644). In an effort to make him "see" she rubs her "stained shoulder and breast against his face" (664) and then runs from the house hysterically, throwing herself in the pool.

Earlier in the story the gardener's dog had accidentally knocked Armitage into the swimming pool, starting a quick train of events that led to his giving up some of his defenses and tenderly making love to Mrs. Johnson. Before her own watery descent she could confess her love for Armitage to the fraud, Smith, but could not say the words to Armitage himself. But now, each having let down the defenses of false pride, the emotional ground is cleared for a deeply sustaining love relationship. The two incidents at the pool are clearly baptisms of a sort, where the psychological stains accompanying the physical afflictions are cleansed. The dual baptisms of a man and a woman, each raised from spiritual desolation and born into a new rich life with each other, are reminiscent of the action of D. H. Lawrence's "The Horse Dealer's Daughter," and the incisive psychological exploration of the effects of blindness on character unmistakably call to mind Lawrence's "The Blind Man." Likewise, the scenes in which Mrs. Johnson tries to make Armitage feel her "insult" or in which he makes her rub spittle and dirt into his eyes have, like scenes out of Lawrence, nothing of the ridiculous about them but are instead somehow realistically convincing even while conveying the aura of sacred mystery and the sacrament of human personality. Although Pritchett does not have Lawrence's depth, his breathtakingly quick and original grasp, or his poetry, "Blind Love" is high enough in quality to render neither author insulted by the comparison.

✛

"The Nest Builder" is also about love completely turning a life around. Psychological revelation is dropped early on, though, in favor of amusement and the ever-so-sly wink.

The story concerns two smart interior decorators, each of them snobs about style. Their words—and the story is told by one of them—suggest that they have a certain delicate sensibility, but Pritchett keeps his humor very dry and perhaps more delicious (but dryness is a matter of taste) by providing no statement or overly direct hint about the sexual orientation of these two longtime partners in the decorating business. One of them, Ernest, the nonnarrator, scores enormous success after success with his female clients: he understands "what most men forget—that women are not merely female; they are feminine" (671). Husbands are first tired and then irritated by Ernest because he rearranges their lives; wives come to adore him and nearly suffer nervous breakdowns when their contracted time is up. Sometimes, for all the elaborate work Ernest does in helping a wife build the perfect nest, her marriage breaks up or her husband forces her to cast aside the fruits of Ernest's labor.

Pritchett has prepared fertile ground for an interesting sociological and psychological study, but he soon reveals, by quick plot manipulation, that he has been after the terribly wry joke all along. Suddenly, much to the chagrin and gaping wonder of the narrator, Ernest meets the "right girl": incredibly, she is heavy-set, ruddy, outdoorsy, and blunt; she redecorates Ernest into a minor country squire, happy amid dogs, cows, and livestock journals. The premise of the joke—that Ernest could be so thoroughly transformed by the love of a woman, and such a woman as this—is rather thin, but the amusement comes, of course, precisely because the style is slickly matter-of-fact, Pritchett being blissfully unconcerned about justifying the implausibility of it all. The joke in the story is so deftly stylized, so knowing, so nonblatant and nonmalicious that it may not (despite Pritchett's proclivity to indulge in some sly humor at the expense of gays) be found especially offensive.

✤

"The Cage Birds," about two sisters, each of whom lives in her own type of prison, came out of Pritchett's memory of two sisters he had known in Paris years before. He had not previously drawn on this material because he "did not know that the creative impulse is often ignited when scenes and people from the almost forgotten past are struck like a flint against something from the present" (*MO*, 23).

While each fictive sister pities the indignity of the other's position, each remains willfully blind to the bars of her own cage. One, Elsie, has the most expensive of clothes and material possessions and thus thinks often of them; the other, Grace, has them not at all and thus thinks often of them too. Grace, the poor sister, has a husband so cheap that he brushes his suit until "it's no longer dark grey, but a parsimonious gleam" (695). Grace's personality has been so submerged that she has come to see her husband's parsimony as a virtue; she now takes pride in extreme acts of penny-pinching that she would once have regarded as acute embarrassments. Thrift and respectability, the Puritan virtues, come close to defining her, the concern with respectability being typically and rather pathetically revealed in what she says to her small son as they ride up in the elevator to her sister's apartment along with a suspicious porter: "'Take your cap off in the lift when you're with a lady,' she said to the boy, asserting to the porter that she was respectable" (698).

Grace is on a yearly visit to Elsie's apartment, where she is to be given the cast-off dresses of her sister, a wealthy and fashionable woman who is decidedly not respectable, unless not enjoying the way she earns her money can somehow be thought a last token of morality: she giggles to Grace that "When they're doing it—you know what I mean—that's when I do my planning. It gives you time to yourself" (704). Elsie has been kept, it would seem, by a succession of men, but she is not faithful to the man currently keeping her. Elsie seems successful in her deceptions; however, she must take bothersome and sometimes panicky precautions not to get caught, just as she must take other precautions to guard her possessions—the literal bars on the apartment windows—lest she be burglarized as she has been in the past. Grace provides an explanation of the story's title when, on her return, she says to her husband, "I don't envy her. She lives in a cage" (709).

While trying on a gold, cast-off dress at Elsie's, Grace had temporarily seen in the mirror someone who wanted to escape her own drab, mean little cage—she saw a beautiful, sexually alluring woman bathed in a radiant glow. But this image is too unsettling for her. She does what she always does, what her husband bids her do—she sells all the dresses Elsie has given her. Like some of the characters of Joyce's *Dubliners,* she will be forever caught in a trap to which she herself remains blind. The epiphany occurs for the reader, not for Grace.

✤

At about 11,000 words "The Skeleton" is a detailed, ironic, comic, and sometimes poignant portrait of George Clark, its 82-year-old protagonist. George is a boring, egocentric, lifelong bachelor, stubbornly existing behind a whole barricade of self-delusions yet fooling himself into thinking that his is a "life devoted to victory" (713). The old man prides himself on being thin ("I'm a skeleton" [714], he says proudly) but does not recognize how his self-imposed isolation has caused fossilization of his spirit.

George, an art collector and scholar, has had no close human contacts, although years before he came near to forming a genuine friendship with a young painter, Flitestone, now long deceased. They liked each other, but George warned himself off: "You lose something when people like you. You are in danger of being stripped naked and of losing a skin" (721). Although George may or may not be homosexual, he is similar to Lionel Frazier, the emotionally isolated hairdresser of the later "A Careless Widow." The ending of the story is a more serious reprise of the idea of "The Nest Builder," wherein the gay decorator finds happiness in marriage. In "The Skeleton" Flitestone's former mistress Gloria suddenly shows up; in her fifties and by her own estimation sexily plump, Gloria is eager to warm the thin old man. Although George had long been a misogynist, Gloria's efforts are somehow availing, and at the story's end George is no longer the terrifying grouch of his London clubs but a satisfied man being complimented on his healthy looks.

Like all of the stories of *Blind Love*, "The Skeleton" exemplifies the "juxtaposition of opposites," the combination of the "straight and subtle, ironic and devious, serious and extraordinarily funny."[24]

The Old Master

Pritchett's birth year of 1900 makes calculation of his age easy, but, the quality of his fiction remaining remarkably high, readers tend to forget just how old he is. The stories collected in *The Camberwell Beauty and Other Stories* (1975), *On the Edge of the Cliff* (1979), and *A Careless Widow and Other Stories* (1989) are those of an author assured of his range, a now-recognized master who remains nearly at the top of his form. Whether the pleasant-mannered, gracious, and self-confidently modest Pritchett was buoyed by the knighthood he received in 1975, or the accolades that greeted his *Collected Stories* in 1982, is hard to determine, but it seems probable that he was. Pritchett has moved on cheerfully and confidently, providing one of those heartening examples of the artist whose creative powers are virtually undiminished by time.

The Camberwell Beauty and Other Stories

Certainly no one was or is now going to become wealthy by selling short stories to magazines. Pritchett may have felt some satisfaction, though, in being better remunerated than other British writers of short fiction. Of the nine stories of *The Camberwell Beauty* (1974), four first appeared in the *New Yorker* ("The Diver" [originally titled "The Fall"], "Our Wife" [originally titled "The Captain's Daughter"], "The Marvellous Girl," and "The Rescue"), three in the high-paying *Playboy* ("Lady from Guatemala," "Did You Invite Me?," and "The Spree"), and one in *Encounter* ("The Last Throw").

The title story of *The Camberwell Beauty* combines vivid characterization, informed knowledge of the London antiques trade, whimsical humor, psychological character study, and near-allegory about male jealousy and possessiveness in love. Pritchett transforms the bizarre into the symbolic, dreary London suburbs into microcosms for the world at large.

In *London Perceived* Pritchett writes that "the antique trade of London is tough and intimately connected; it shows a head in innumerable districts; it is a collection of tricky eccentrics, watching one another like spies, and it is the least on-coming, the most misleadingly absent-minded trade in London. And why not? A large number of its clientele—I mean the core of the business, not the casual dropper-in—are obsessed or mad."[25] Given this understanding, readers may not find, as did several reviewers, that "The Camberwell Beauty" goes in for the improbable, the fey, or even the fantastic.

The story's narrator is a dealer new to the business, a novice who has not yet decided on his specialty or secret lust. He takes careful note of two of his fellow dealers—August, a collector of ivory, and Pliny, who specializes in Meissen ware (porcelain). In August's shop he sees a teenage girl, Isabel, August's wife's niece, and she is to exert an almost hypnotic hold on him for most of the story. The three male antiques dealers—the narrator, August, and Pliny—all have their lust for rare precious objects, but the lust for possessing the beautiful Isabel is paramount. August, it seems, has tried to steal into her bed but has been repelled, and the narrator has not got to know her well before failing in his trade and thus moving outside the orbit of antiques dealers.

Several years later the narrator, now a real estate auctioneer, has his business take him near the old shops, and he inquires about August and Pliny. He learns to his stupefaction that Isabel is now married to old Pliny, a longtime bachelor and archrival of August. The impotent old man keeps her virtually locked up, and every night he commands her to undress while he looks—simply looks—at her with the same pride of possession he reserves for his most prized porcelain objects. He warns her off all other men, saying they have only, as her Uncle August did, sexual exploitation in mind. When he is not at home he requires her to dress as a soldier, beat a marching drum, and blow a bugle to scare away would-be rapists and seducers. It is perhaps beside the point to ask what Isabel's motivations are. Though an enigmatic figure, she does not especially appear to be a half-wit and may well not be demented in any ordinary sense. She is one of those Pritchett characters who seem lifelike (we see third dimensions in lightninglike flashes), yet we are largely left to guess what her interior life is like. A victim of attempted molestation, she seems content and perhaps even happy in the constant world of the "safe" old man who wants only to worship her as an objet d'art. She tells the narrator "with warmth" (855) and against his objections that what she and Pliny have together is indeed love. And while it at first seems bizarre, the blowing of the bugle might deter urban assault as effectively as many other means. At any rate it kills sexual desire in the narrator when he visits.

The story's theme reverberates long in the mind precisely because Pritchett works successfully at making the story seem real at the literal level. Because it is left to readers' own intelligence and sensitivity to draw all salient points regarding ways in which many men, or even men in general, use women only to satisfy vanity or sexual appetite, this theme has more force than it would had Pritchett directed readers to it more expressly. Readers are compelled to ponder how men's lust for possession violates a woman's selfhood and reduces her to a thing even as it reduces the humanity of her predator, acting at an animal level. It suggests too, as does John Fowles's first novel, *The Collector,* that collectors, if not already dead in spirit, metaphorically kill themselves in their mania for collecting.

✢

"The Marvellous Girl," a story that provides atmosphere and emotionally charged moments more than character and plot, causes the reader to think about modern relationships between the sexes vis-à-vis the old questions about delusion, compatibility and incompatibility, and romantic attraction. The protagonist is a young painter named Francis, a divorced man whose situation is common among modern people of the artistic and professional classes: "More than two years had gone by since he and his wife had lived together. The marriage was one of those prickly friendships that never succeeded—to *his* astonishment at any rate—in turning into love, but are kept going by curiosity. It had become at once something called 'our situation': a duet by a pair of annoyed hands" (898). As Francis, the focal character in a limited omniscient narrative, thinks about the kind of life led by his ex-wife after their divorce, some readers will be reminded of people they know in real life; others will think of characters in Iris Murdoch novels: "My wife had broken with that wretched man Duncan who had gone off with a girl called Irmgard, and when my wife heard of it she made him throw Irmgard over and took him back, and once she'd got him she took up with the Professor" (902).

The ex-wife (her name is never given) sounds both superficial and neurotic, but we can by no means be sure—the narrator confines us to Francis's judgments and perceptions. On the other hand, Francis's life since the divorce seems sterile; he has immersed himself in work and has no emotional involvements. But one night he runs into his ex-wife at a restaurant; with her is a young woman who is her co-worker at an art institute. This young secretary gives him a radiant smile and a beguiling "good-bye," and sets off in Francis an almost chemical reaction. To him she becomes simply "the marvellous girl." From this moment on the story maintains a successful double-edged effect. Readers can share the excitement of Francis's romantic infatuation, or they can view it ironically. They may in fact be able to do both at the same time, as Pritchett walks the fine line between romance and gentle mockery all the way through to the end of the story.

Francis decides to attend a presentation in the auditorium of the art institute, knowing that the marvelous girl will be there with his ex-wife. He sits in the audience, the pulse of romance beating warm and fast, in the hope of being able to make contact with the young woman. He feels an almost feverish need to find her, and readers share his feeling of tension, a feeling sustained for well over 2,000 words, interrupted only by flashbacks that fill us in on the relationship between him and his ex-wife. The tension reaches a climax as the lights in the auditorium fail and Francis, in blind love for the marvelous girl and clear-eyed aversion to his ex-wife, pushes his way through the exiting crowd in what now seems a desperate hope of finding the newly beloved before she leaves. Although the darkness is relieved only by the lighted matches held by some in the crowd, the young woman somehow sees him and calls out his name—indeed, the first time the name Francis is given. Almost at once they are a team with interlaced fingers, hoping to avoid being sighted by Francis's ex-wife. They succeed in this, although the ex-wife passes by so closely that the buttons on her coat momentarily interlock with those of Francis's, a delicate, unforced symbol. Their marriage too was largely the result of their accidentally being thrown together, and it proved an awkward, frictional experience, a nasty if quite temporary snag in two people's lives. The release of the buttons signals the real end of an emotionally damaging relationship.

Francis takes the marvelous girl to the director's suite, and they are locked in a passionate embrace on the sofa just as the lights are restored. But they have had time to declare their love to each other and, suffused with their romantic glow, move out into the street to be embraced by the darkness of the city.

One of many Pritchett stories on which commentators are divided, "The Marvellous Girl" illustrates well a general divergence of opinion. Anatole Broyard, on the one hand, feels Pritchett too inclined merely to *"present the mystery of character"* rather than *"plucking out [its] heart."* "The story gives you a few clues and the rest is up to you," Broyard complains about many Pritchett stories. He adds that "The Marvellous Girl" and "Our Wife" "don't even live up to the requirements of this particular genre. They are too thin: There are no interstices for us to work in, not enough pieces for the jigsaw puzzle."[26]

On the other hand, many commentators agree that Pritchett involves the reader in the interpretive process in an unusually demanding way but see this as no deficiency. Dean Baldwin, also using a jigsaw-puzzle comparison, expresses the admiring view of "The Marvellous Girl": "It is easy to miss or minimize the technical perfection. . . . The narrative elements have to be fitted together like pieces in an elaborate puzzle without interfering with the emotional shades and nuances to create a moment at which one relationship ends and another is born. Both purposes must be satisfied without elaborate exposition. Beyond the technical perfection of the story are the human and thematic elements that make us care about these characters. This is a short story for connoisseurs" (Baldwin, 89).

✦

"The Rescue" and "The Diver" recount the sexual initiations of young men, each of them inhibited puritans. "The Diver" is by far the more consequential of the two, although "The Rescue," whose narrator is a highly sexed 16-year-old excited about owning "the shortest mini-skirt in town" (886), is genuinely amusing. The initiate, a "boy of twenty," is the most comically extreme of all Pritchett's puritans: he advocates that people caught in adultery be given the same punishment as Hester Prynne (888–89).

"The Diver" has an autobiographical basis, undoubtedly the reason it reflects a greater and more convincing particularity of detail than "The Rescue" does. The nameless, first-person narrator of "The Diver," a young Englishman in Paris, is much like the young Pritchett autobiographically revealed in *Midnight Oil*. Both are aspiring writers, both work in the leather trade in Paris, and both, despite the mockery of their co-workers, are proud of their virginity. The narrator of "The Diver," telling his story from the vantage point of a time long after the events described, says, "I not only admitted I hadn't gotten a mistress, but boasted about it. To the office boys this news was extravagant. It doubled them up" (858).

An initiation story, "The Diver" contains, as do most stories of its kind, a fair amount of symbolism and at least a hint of myth and allegory. The connection between sex and artistic creativity is the one most intriguingly offered for our attention. The protagonist fiercely desires to be a writer yet is blocked at a very early stage—he does not know what to write about. Both his sexual and artistic problems are, however, largely solved on the same day. A barge containing a consignment of dressed skins, bound for the firm he works for, has been sunk in the Seine. Their employer sends the narrator and another man down to the quay to inspect the bales of skins for damage as a salvage team brings them to the surface. For a week the narrator enjoys watching the diver who is chiefly responsible for getting the sodden cargo to the surface, but on the last day the narrator is accidentally knocked into the cold darkness of the Seine.

This accident turns out to be fortuitous, for it precipitates a chain of events that lead the narrator to sexual and, we are led to suppose, artistic fulfillment. A symbolic baptism of sorts, it reminds one of the dual baptisms in "Blind Love," wherein Armitage and Mrs. Johnson are born into fuller lives after immersion in a swimming pool.

The symbolism in "The Diver" is even more intricate and expert than this, however. The experience is the sign or correlative of the narrator's coming to terms with the instinctual or animal (the "skin") part of himself; it appears to effectuate a reintegration of personality for the young man. Cécile Oumhani points out that

> The fall into the water is associated with animals, through the appearance of the diver who had been hired to rescue the cargo and whom the narrator had been watching too closely when he fell. The diver is described as looking "like a swollen frog" [861]. The skins contained in the barge, which the diver was busy bringing up, are actually parts of animals, and the shape they take when hung to dry on poles is said to evoke both animals and human beings: "It was like hanging up drowned animals—even, I thought, human beings" [861]. The diver, looking like an animal, and the skins associate human beings and animals. It is as if the narrator were recovering a part of himself that had remained repressed before, as if he were recognizing a more instinctive aspect of his nature, after his plunge into the darker regions, symbolized by water.[27]

The rite of passage is completed for the young, shivering narrator when Mme Chamson, who does business with his employer, decides to provide a change of clothes for him. She is a woman of rather imperious mien who easily cows the narrator. She orders him to undress, and the young man is embarrassed to find that he has an erection in front of this 40-year-old, very commanding woman. Before, though, when he had seen her at his employer's place of business, she had seemed a "ribald, coquettish, dangerous woman who came wagging her hips" (864); now she seems merely concerned about his health. He does not feel threatened by lurid or defiling sexuality, and his natural urges are released. She pretends to be insulted by his obvious excitement, and her ample "bosom [becomes] a bellows puffing outrage" (864).

Soon, though, she beckons him to a farther room, which turns out to be a bedroom, where he finds her lying provocatively nude. She correctly senses that he has had no experience, and she taunts him for it. Finally tired about being teased about his sexual innocence, he fabricates a story about how, when he was 12 years old, he found a naked woman shopkeeper murdered in her bed. Mme Chamson seems quite suitably impressed by this story, but soon she is pulling at the narrator's trousers, saying "The diver's come up again. Forget. Forget" (869). Her metaphor of the diver shows us how Pritchett had used subsumed sexual imagery earlier in the story to suggest that the narrator was on the verge of being able to accept his identity as a creature partly sexual. The narrator had previously identified himself with the young, vigorous diver whose repeated divings figured the sexual act. Pascal Aquien points out that "the diver, described as a kind of he-man—'the hero of the week' [860]—or gallant soldier with his 'round helmet' [860], is associated with another phallic image, that of the crane moving up and down. Moreover, the boy insists on the 'swollen' aspect of the diver. Active and efficient as he is, 'in the river bed' [860], which is here more than a mere geographical description, he is wholly virile."[28]

The story's adumbration of the somewhat mysterious but often speculated about linkage of creativity (here the improvised story about the murder) and sexuality carries a quality of conviction; the sharp evocation of the Paris of the 1920s creates an atmosphere that is both thematically appropriate and colorful.

✣

"The Spree" and "The Lady from Guatemala" are both successful, although in different seriocomic ways. In "The Spree" Pritchett treats the ache of loneliness in an elderly London widower in a way that is gently comedic yet also poignant and sympathetic. Bereft of friends and contemporaries, the old man takes himself on a day's outing that is unfulfilling until he is accidentally swept into a bus chartered to carry a group of young people to the seashore. He is fortunate not only in having the convivial company of the young but also in establishing a relationship with a "stowaway" on the bus—a woman near his own age. The story contains the repeated theme of the importance of relationships in sustaining the spirit, particularly in old age.

"The Lady from Guatemala" is another story about love and need, mixing comedy and emotionally painful feelings in a way that makes the reader feel slightly guilty about enjoying the humor. The focal character, Julian Drood, is a leftist newspaper editor whose liberalism has never really been tested until an adoring and hero-worshiping Indian lady from Guatemala comes to throw herself at his feet. Although Drood honestly believes he is free of racism, sexism, and prejudice of any sort, his first view of the lady from Guatemala immediately suggests to the reader how sorely his surface ideals are going to be tried: "At first because of her tweed hat, he thought she was a man and would have said she had a mustache. She was a stump, as square as a box, with tarry, chopped-off hair, heavy eyebrows and yellow eyes set in her sallow skin like cut glass. She looked like some unsexed and obdurate statement about the future—or was it the beginning?—of the human race, long in the body, short in the legs and made of wood" (939).

An initial reader reaction will be to find Drood's profound discomfiture simply but amply amusing, but then those readers will embarrassedly come to recognize that they, like Drood, are regarding the lady from Guatemala as a bizarre, laughable entity rather than a noble-minded, emotionally and spiritually rich human being, ridiculous only in hailing the fallible Drood as "liberator" and "Godhead" (945). A gradual epiphany occurs for the reader sometime earlier than it does for Drood, a character whom many of us might come to see as rather uncomfortably like ourselves.

✦

"Did You Invite Me?" is a low-key, comic exploration of the general theme of all the stories in the collection—the strange congeries of forces that initially bring and later bind men and women together. Mutual friends introduce a middle-aged widower to a divorcée of about the same age, but, because both are self-conscious and defensive about their own weaknesses, they tend to find each other stilted and boring. An emotional turning point occurs in the story when they meet by accident in the park and their dogs get into a bloody fight. Each seems to come to recognize that people do not always present the best side of themselves, that people have hidden depths and unspoken virtues. The end of the story finds them living together in a solid relationship; they have apparently made concessions and compromises, both private and mutual, so that they can have the kind of relationship each one needs.

On the Edge of the Cliff

On the Edge of the Cliff (1979) collects nine stories, nearly all of them dealing with extramarital love and passion. Thematically, several raise the question of whether romantic love involves only deception or if it can involve the stripping away of the inessentials that lie between a person's surface and the very core of his or her being.

Pritchett had done well with the sales of these stories, several of them having dual publication in American and British magazines. Again the *New Yorker* led the way with three; two were published in *Encounter*, and one each appeard in the *Atlantic*, *Playboy*, and the *New Statesman*, among other periodicals.

✤

The best of these is the title story, an understated story of a "seventyish" widower involved in a mutual love relationship with an attractive, 25-year-old woman. One might expect that this basic situation would incline the treatment toward either the heavily ironic or the sentimental, but Pritchett takes neither path. A call for judgment—either moral or intellectual—is not what the story is about.

Harry is a retired professor and botanist; Rowena, his mistress, is an artist. They live in his house on a remote hillside near the sea, a stark landscape that suggests the timelessness of nature and death. In some ways Harry is a crotchety old man. Of a country fair he says, "It's no good. Plastic, like cheap food. Not worth seeing. The twentieth century has packaged everything" (959). Still, he knows his unusual relationship needs careful management: "There are rules for old men who are in love with young girls, all the stricter when the young girls are in love with them. It has to be played as a game" (957). One rule is that neither should ever make any reference to the age gap. Another rule Harry makes for himself is that he should never allow himself to be seen naked by Rowena in daylight. Readers may smile at this odd couple's games, but the author seems to suggest that everyone who is really alive is involved in some form of game; rules—and perhaps also illusions—make life psychologically bearable.

Harry is of an age that causes him (as we see when we are briefly in his consciousness) to be dominated by thoughts of death; each hour he spends with Rowena pulls him toward life, but he can still feel the tug of the final reality, every bit as strong as the pull of gravity. Harry is very much on the edge of the cliff. The one real incident in the story consciously reinforces this awareness for him. He meets by chance a middle-aged widow, Daisy, an old friend, accompanied by Stephen, a young man he assumes is her son. Harry is thoroughly shaken to find that the young man, who is about the same age as Rowena, is not the woman's son at all but her lover. This confrontation with a mirror image of their own relationship causes Rowena too a temporary shock: "'You can't mean that,' she said, putting on a very proper air. 'She's old enough—' but she stopped, and instead of giving him one of her light hugs, she rumpled his hair" (973). Although Rowena's rumpling of the hair is loving and reassuring, it has an unconscious touch of condescension in it, as if Rowena (whose mind we never really see inside) wants to be almost a maternal protectress to a weakening old man beginning to feel something of the powerlessness of childhood.

As he does so often, Pritchett causes his reader to walk a tightrope of emotional responses. Unless readers are being consciously analytical they are not apt to notice how the author is affecting them by a subtle modulation of tones, taking them from hard-edged realism to pathos to poetic celebration to comic deflation and back again. One could scornfully smile at Harry, feel pathos for him, or view him with admiration. Harry's attempt to defeat time is quixotic to be sure, but most readers will probably admire him for it more than not. One illustrative scene might etch itself in the reader's memory. To prove something to himself and Rowena, Harry takes her along the seaside cliffs to a dangerous cove, a place of hard-breaking surf, rocks, and deep icy water. Breaking his own rule about never being naked before Rowena in daylight, he strips and stands there, "belly wrinkled" and "thighs shrunk" (966), hands lifted for his dive. A memorable scene, it seems little more a testimony to an indomitable part of the human spirit than a sheer piece of foolhardiness. And indeed he does dive, and swim far out, thoroughly terrifying Rowena. That night "he [is] astounded when she [comes] into his room and [gets] into his bed: she had not done this before. 'I've come to see the Ancient Mariner'" (967), she says. (The danger of drowning, associated with the release of sexual energies involving partners widely separated in age, recalls "The Diver," although we have here a last hurrah rather than an initiation.) The story is a kind of poetic meditation on Eros and Thanatos, but, far from being anything like a reductive psychological parable, it stimulates meditation on the needs and aspirations of the human spirit in a finite and imperfect world.

✦

Deceptions in love are involved in both "The Accompanist" and "The Fig Tree." In fact, in both stories the narrator is well known to a husband he is cuckolding. These stories, like some others, implicitly ask some questions about the ways people "invent" themselves, "invent" people close to them, and "invent" relationships.

The central character in "The Accompanist" is a musical accompanist, but the metaphoric implications of the title (like those of "The Diver" and "The Skeleton") demand to be considered. In what ways are some people apt to be accompanists to those who go off on jaunts in pursuit of private whims, or even accompanists to those who go off on lifelong quests prompted by some basic delusion?

Joyce, the adulterous young wife, likes to think of herself as someone in the process of inventing herself, but in fact other people invent her—she is just naturally an accompanist. One evening as Joyce and her husband entertain friends at home, she plays the piano as an accompaniment to her husband's singing. The narrator, William, her partner in adultery and friend of her husband, remarks that "she sang and she played as if she did not exist" (1056). The source of her "absence" is mysterious. It seems that she married Bertie simply because he asked her to, although in most ways the proposal came out of the blue. She has grown to love Bertie, despite that the two of them are apparently husband and wife in name only. She has confessed poor Bertie's inadequacies to William, and this violation of her husband's privacy fills her alternately with remorse and a kind of thrill—this night particularly, because William is in the room. Probably as a psychological cover for his sexual incapacity, Bertie heartily sings a few bawdy French songs, and Joyce, at the piano, flashes several ironic looks at her lover.

Bertie, orphaned barely out of infancy, not only does not hide his need for human connection but even extorts sympathy from time to time. It would seem that this quality had something to do with the reason for Joyce's consenting to marry him. William says, "He was a rarity, and our rarity too. We were a kind of society for cosseting him. Joyce, who loved him, felt this, and I did too" (1055).

Bertie is sexually impotent with Joyce, but whether he would be with all women is something we cannot know. Possibly, he subconsciously identifies Joyce with his long-dead mother, and the incest taboo renders him sexually incapable. At one point William thinks that Joyce's "look told me that I could never know how truly she loved Bertie and feared him too, as she would love and fear a child" (1059). Then too, Bertie may be a repressed (or even self-recognized) homosexual. But it is not totally "unfair" for readers to be given insufficient means for making a determination. Joyce presumably does not know the reason for her husband's impotence, and possibly Bertie does not consciously know it either.

A small network of bone imagery appears in the story, although all of it presented through William, the narrator; he thinks, for example, that he "had advanced to the fantasy that when [Joyce] laughed, her collarbones laughed" and that she has "the look of a girl who has a strange shame on her bones" (1056). William seems to desire a kind of psychological X-ray machine—to know people in their very bones. Such a wish will obviously be frustrated. William does come to a discovery about himself, if not about

Bertie; William has a flash of insight that he himself is an accompanist, not one of the main performers. He is suddenly jealous of Bertie and Joyce: "Their talk of food, money, their daily domestic life, was irritating in my situation. I lived by my desire; they had the intimacy of eating" (1059). With his own career in Singapore, he probably has the feeling of being a man very much on the periphery, a useful instrument someone will push on stage to provide an accompaniment. Ironically, the title may refer more to him than to Joyce.

✦

"The Fig Tree" is a humorous story with more than a hint, however, of the Jamesian touch. Like "The Accompanist," the story is told by a narrator who is cuckolding a husband who is a friend, although in this story we cannot be sure what subtleties or intricacies of thought may be going on in the minds of the husband and Sally, the wife, or even their 14-year-old daughter.

Sally calls in the narrator, Teddy, a nurseryman, to look after a dying fig tree, soon recognized as emblematic of her sexual life because she has not slept with her husband, Duggie, since the birth of their daughter. (Figs have long been connected with female sexuality; the dying fig tree might, with oblique irony, suggest the barren fig tree cursed by Christ in the gospels.) Sally and Teddy are soon involved in a love affair, but Duggie, who must travel to the Continent often, concocts his own quiet, ironic, effective revenge. He sends his daughter, who also has a crush on Teddy, abroad to a boarding school and arranges for Sally to work at the nursery. As Duggie foresees, the daily working relationship of Sally and Teddy is fatal to their affair, a mutual feeling of bored domesticity soon settling in. At the end Teddy is plaintively meditating that "the roles of Duggie and myself were reversed: when Duggie came home once a week now from Brussels it was he who seemed to be the lover and I the husband" (1109). As in "The Accompanist," the husband gains an ultimate triumph of sorts.

✦

Christine Jackson in "The Wedding" is self-assured and prim on the outside but harbors ambivalent feelings of various kinds within; some of these arise because she has, in a phrase Pritchett uses in several stories, "invented herself." She tells a fellow teacher, a male, that she sees nothing wrong in girls wanting to be duchesses: "Why shouldn't they think they are duchesses? I always wanted to be one. Girls are practical. A girl is a new thing: they have to invent themselves" (1006).

Back after many years in her home village, the divorced, 30-year-old Mrs. Jackson gives off an air of foreign mystery and more sophisticated worlds, causing the villagers to invent her in *their* fantasies. She attends a wedding at which sexual undercurrents are strong, and becomes unwillingly a part of a local custom of the earthy farmers, being lassoed, as other women are, by one of the men. Mrs. Jackson is understandably indignant. But the ritual enactment of basic life forces and urges is a dramatically powerful, almost Lawrentian, moment. In an understated and carefully selective manner, Pritchett allows readers to feel the social and sexual antagonisms that exist between the farmer and the teacher, the ebb and flow of opposed feelings so clearly reminiscent of Lawrence. That the story ends with the farmer winning her heart does not, because of Pritchett's deft management, seem either sentimental or hackneyed.

The dramatic pace of "The Wedding" and its visually imagined central action seem to make it a natural for the stage or film, and it in fact was filmed for British television. Although not totally satisfied, Pritchett liked the production, noting that "they caught the note of frolic you need if you are going to describe a country wedding: the air of genial lust and general horseplay" (Forkner and Séjourné, 37).

A Careless Widow and Other Stories

The publication of *A Careless Widow and Other Stories* (1989) coincided almost exactly with Pritchett's eighty-ninth birthday. In this collection of six stories Pritchett makes telling use of patented styles and techniques, without seeming to repeat himself unduly.

✦

The title story is redolent of Joyce's "A Painful Case" in both theme and technique, except that Pritchett is not so scrupulously mean or so dramatic in his handling of epiphany. Pritchett's story is more open in form and his character observation gentler, although he again slightly indulges in arch humor arising from the plight of the timid homosexual.

The protagonist is Lionel Frazier, a confirmed bachelor and popular hairdresser at a smart London salon. A man of regular and meticulous habit, Frazier keeps a "perfect kitchen," takes pride in his skill as a chic amateur interior decorator, and owns a prized velvet sofa. Aside, though, from the culinary delights of his kitchen and the relative opulence of his living room, he appears to live a rather spartan life. His only indulgence is an annual holiday to the southwestern corner of England, where beneath a "young and ageless" sky amid a "rocky land [that] got older every day" he feels "re-born" (1120).

The story opens as Frazier—apparently in his late fifties—is staying at his customary hotel somewhere near Falmouth. He is horrified to discover that Mrs. Morris, the careless widow who has the apartment immediately below his in London, is also a guest at the hotel. Although she seemed at first a respectable enough woman, she is associated in Lionel's mind with "mess." Once she had even spilled a few drops of whiskey on his velvet sofa, necessitating a complete reupholstering ("The expense!" [1119]). Part of Lionel likes Mrs. Morris, but altogether he is unnerved by her and by the importunate visits she began to pay him after the death of the man she lived with: "She was ordinary life and ordinary life always went too far" (1119), he thinks. Once as he listened to her, Frazier became very aware that "Mrs. Morris was a body," and he realizes that his own tendency is to find this prospect strange and somewhat repellent: "His clientele were no more than heads that he gardened as he gardened the plants on his balcony" (1116).

The greatest divide between Frazier and Mrs. Morris is that "she was deep in the belief in the plural quality of the first person singular" (1116). Frazier's life, on the other hand, almost defines the singular quality of the first person singular. He is at least a fraternal twin of the Dubliner James Duffy, who lives a life he thinks antiseptically pure until events force him to see the pathos of his loneliness and emotional sterility. Both fictional characters construct elaborate facades of orderliness as a protective mechanism against an aggravated sense of the disorder in their emotional lives. Frazier does not have the heavily defined epiphany of Duffy, but he does come to a fleeting realization at the conclusion of the story. As the widow leaves for the last time, Frazier ruefully thinks, "Another garrulous fragment of ordinary life was leaving him, going about its business. He was afloat in space, and below him he began to feel the cold air of an empty flat" (1126). Spiritually the affable Frazier is dead, and it is no accident that his favorite rock formation along the seaside cliffs is known as "the Coffin."

No reviewer seems to have remarked that the story is about the plight of the chaste homosexual who has ruinously repressed his emotional life along with his sexuality. When in an interview Pritchett labeled Frazier "a sort of homosexual" (Forkner and Séjourné, 29), he seems to have spoken unguardedly. But the reviewers' reluctance to label has a reason: Pritchett's general respect for the individuality and amplitude of his characters is at complete odds with overdefined or reductive interpretations.

❖

"Cocky Olly," the best story in the collection, is an initiation story that has poetry, insight, emotion, and a clear but by no means diagrammatically simple definition of its theme. The events of the story show a young girl's breaking through a doubly protective cocoon in which she had been kept by her parents.

Fourteen-year-old Sarah comes to awareness of herself and life as she becomes more deeply acquainted with the liberal and eccentric Short family, who live on the adjoining property. Until this time Sarah had existed within the tight, closed circle of mother and father. Her absurdly reactionary father may at first seem a cartoon along the lines of the famous Colonel Blimp of David Low, but such caricatures reflected real life and had to magnify and exaggerate only slightly. Although Sarah's father scarcely knows the Shorts, he fulminates about them: "Weekend riffraff.... Gang of traitors. Pacifists, long-haired pansies, atheists, bathing stark naked in that swimming-pool. Friends of Hitler and Stalin. Calls himself a major" (1128–29). Sarah's father had been a brigadier in World War I, had been wounded, and lost a hand. His maiming has caused him bitterness; his brush with death has caused him to fear life as well as death. In part he is jealous of the Shorts, who are not as eccentric as he would like to think—not only do they not bathe naked in their pool; they do not even have a pool.

Sarah, now a schoolteacher, tells the story retrospectively, 40 years after the events occur. The story's tone combines the nostalgia and wistfulness of the narrator with the wonder, joy, vitality, confusion, and coming-to-awareness of her much younger self. Her passage into the real world of openness and complexity is effectuated chiefly by Sarah's acquaintance with Benedict Short, two years younger than she, a mischievous, artistic, maladjusted boy. At his house the two of them, accompanied by many other children, play Cocky Olly, a game much like Prisoner's Base. They race about the house, shouting and flinging open doors, but Mr. and Mrs. Short are perfectly and easily tolerant. The opening of doors is an apt metaphor for what Sarah's new friendship with the Shorts is doing for her life: "At home we lived to ourselves, as my father said. Doors were always shut in our house. Here [in the Short house] all the doors were open and names were flying about" (1135).

Although Hitler and Stalin are not among them, the Shorts have a wide circle of friends and acquaintances, and the air is alive with excitement, possibility, and the joy of the yet undiscovered. Sarah breathes in this rich air, and the lungs of her soul fill and expand.

The story does, though, maintain its realistic contours; it is not just a happy, romantic parable about psychological expansion and liberation, or an adult's nostalgically selective memory of the events of youth. The Shorts are not fully equated with happiness and freedom. Benedict is a neurotic boy who repeatedly runs away from his boarding school and retreats to private worlds of his own. Major Short's laying heavy bets on the horses seems to signify not so much that he is open to life and unafraid of chance as that he has some need to escape an inner emptiness, perhaps associated with the suicidal drowning years before (1143) of his first wife (she was abandoned by a lover with whom she had run away) or with his own serious wounding in World War I. Sarah's passage from innocence to experience involves her coming to terms with the world as it really is—being able to accept it in its ambiguities and complexities. The world of the Shorts is more liberating than that of Sarah's parents, but she intuits correctly that she must integrate the order and predictability represented by her father with the exuberance and spontaneity represented by Major Short. After all, even the exuberant game of Cocky Olly ("all of us racing around" [1154]) has its rules.

✦

Although comedy and irony of several kinds play their roles in "A Change of Policy," the story allows itself some explicit indulgence of softer feelings, a phenomenon relatively rare in Pritchett. Paula, the protagonist, is like Lionel Frazier of "A Careless Widow" in that she does not "like messes" (131). But because of "a change of policy" the scholarly journal for which she works lets her go, and her self-esteem rapidly deteriorates until she allows herself, in a personal change of policy, to become romantically involved with George, a printer. George's wife has been in a coma for more than two years, and Paula begins to become, after the boy's initial resentment, a kind of surrogate mother to George's son.

The surprise in this story is that at this point Pritchett seems to embark on his own change of policy. The story becomes unembarrassedly contrived and sentimental, perhaps in a deliberately old-fashioned way. George is killed in a fall from a horse, his widow suddenly comes out of her coma, and Paula steps forward to care for widow and son; they live under the same roof in a harmonious relationship. The story is a departure for Pritchett in that it allows the play of tender emotion, which is, however, largely canceled by the melodramatic contrivance Pritchett, perhaps half-winkingly, builds in. In some loose and imprecise way Pritchett may have intended subsumed ironies to balance the sentimentality, but the design remains flawed.

+

"The Image Trade" is both a jeu d'esprit and a half-serious meditation on literary art as it is practiced by an eminent literary man much like Pritchett himself. As Pearson, the elderly author, endures a photographic session at his home at the hands of the noted photographer Zut, he is forcibly reminded that both of them are in the "image trade." "The famous Zut" (1211) is reputed to be an artist with his camera, not just "one of your click-click men" (1218). Pearson tries a small bit of humorous dueling with Zut, but Zut's approach is no-nonsense and almost dour. (This quality may account for his name, Zut, a French exclamation meaning something very much like "Go to the Devil!") Zut is assisted by his wife, to whom he gives countless little punches and pushes when she does not anticipate his wishes quickly enough. The elderly subject, a veteran of many photo sessions, becomes a bit uneasy and thinks, "Talk, Zut. All photographers talk, put client at ease. Ask me questions" (1213). But Zut speaks only when necessary. Pearson's humorous observations on the whole process become—given Zut's granite impassivity—unspoken and are shared only by the reader. As he wonderingly contemplates Zut's method, Pearson thinks, "You're not like that man who came here last year and told me that he waited until he felt there was a magnetic flow uniting himself and me. A technological flirt. Nor are you like that other happy fellow with the waving hair who said he unselfed himself, forgot money, wife, children, all, for a few seconds, to become me!" (1216).

Pearson wonders why Zut does not try to find the essence of his personality or art by questioning him or entertaining his own suggestions. Instead Zut simply poses Pearson the way he (Zut) wants. At the end of the story, when Pearson goes to an exhibition of Zut's photographs, he sees why: Zut's photographic portrait of Pearson "had portrayed his soul instead of mine" (1218). Despite his indignation, Pearson must wonder at another level whether he as a literary artist does not do much the same thing as Zut. Although his characters may proceed from real people whom he has observed from the outside, are they not animated and motivated by aspects of Pearson's own personality? Is every work of art not, to some degree at least, an act of self-exposure? And in a broader question, one that applies not just to the artist but to everyone, can one separate "essence" from "image"? As Zut was photographing him, Pearson had thought of earlier selves revealed in photographs, and he must wonder to what extent some of these selves were created by vanity, fashion, or other ephemeral motives: "There was my Popular Front look in the Thirties and Forties, the jersey-wearing, all-the-world's-a-coal-mine period. . . . There was the editorial look, when the tailor had to let out the waist of my trousers, followed by the successful smirk. In the Sixties the plunging neckline, no tie. Then back to collar and tie in my failed-bronze-Olympic period. Today I fascinate archaeologists—you know the broken look of a lost civilisation" (1213).

Zut is Pearson's ironic double, and there is the teasing suggestion that Pritchett himself, humorously self-deprecatory, is their triplet. His own house is much like Pearson's, and Pritchett, like his fictional counterpart, writes on a board rather than a desk or table. Pearson thinks, "There are tons of me left. I know I have a face like a cup of soup with handles sticking out—you know?—after it has been given a couple of stirs with a wooden spoon. A specialty in a way. What wouldn't I give for bone structure, a nose with bone in it!" (1217). Pritchett seems to suggest a self-deprecating parallel between Pearson's face and his own. Like Zut, Sir Victor does not drive a car (nor has he ever done so), and, like Zut, he has been constantly and valuably assisted in his profession by his wife, Dorothy (to whom he probably does not, however, give hard nudges and shoves). Pearson calls Zut an "unfortunate Satan walking up and down the world looking for souls" (1216). And Pritchett too has roamed his various worlds looking for souls to populate his fiction. Still, Pritchett is no Satan—he is a benevolent god who showers the people of his world with constant understanding and compassion.

The Writer's Palette

When readers of Pritchett's stories are asked to quickly recall his chief themes, they are bound to think first of eccentricity, self-delusion, puritanism, loneliness, and spiritual isolation.[29] These are indeed the dominant thematic areas, but any attempt at rigorous classification presents difficulties and is only moderately useful. Pritchett's range is wider than first impressions may suggest, and his delicately nuanced themes and characters resist any overtly schematic categorization. Moreover, Pritchett himself is uncomfortable with the categorization of his stories by theme or character type, for he hopes his characters have been invested with enough individuality and enough of the illusion of freedom and unpredictability that they defy such classification. He has said that "the novelists' or the short story writers' duty is to destroy generalization. . . . All human beings are different and I want to see the distinctions. There is something that takes them outside the generality" (Forkner and Séjourné, 30).

❖

The success of "Cocky Olly," the best story of the 1989 *A Careless Widow*, may remind readers of Pritchett's other initiation stories. "The Saint" (*IMNH*) is the most notable, and Pritchett's own favorite among all his stories, "When My Girl Comes Home" (*WMGCH*), may justifiably be labeled an initiation story. Another successful one is "The Diver" (*CB*); others include "The Clerk's Tale" (*IMNH*) and "The Rescue" (*CB*). All of these involve the passage from innocence to experience; however, they differ greatly in coloration and method of development.

Although with varied degrees of thematic centrality, a number of stories delineate the ways in which business and the business ethic can cause the human soul to shrivel or the mind to become distorted. The three best of these have a thematic depth and breadth that take them well beyond a simplistic antibusiness stance, even pushing the implied critique to the background: "Sense of Humour" (*YMYOL*), "It May Never Happen" (*IMNH*), and "The Camberwell Beauty" (*CB*). Others include "The White Rabbit" (*SV*), "The Upright Man (*YMYOL*), "Page and Monarch" (*YMYOL*), "The Chestnut Tree" (*IMNH*), "The Liars" (*BL*), "The Chain-

Smoker" (*BL*), "The Last Throw" (*CB*), and "The Worshippers" (*OEC*).

Themes of puritanism are, of course, often allied with the theme of business, but some of the stories that deal most directly with "Puritan" characters are "The Sailor" (*IMNH*), "Handsome Is as Handsome Does" (*YMYOL*), "It May Never Happen" (*IMNH*), and "The Cage Birds" (*BL*). Other, less significant stories in this group are "The Cuckoo Clock" (*SV*) and "The Rescue" (*CB*).

It often seems that social class preoccupies the English almost obsessively. Class has a relatively significant role to play in Pritchett's short fiction, but it is not what his stories are "about." He writes not so much about class as about what people come to discover about their own characters as they enact certain class gestures or devote fascinated attention to class "markers." Pritchett, who always pays minute attention to those details he selects for inclusion, renders social nuances subtly and precisely. Relatively few of the stories place delineations of class differences on an equal footing with depiction of individual character. One group that does, however, is composed of the three stories of *The Key to My Heart*—"The Key to My Heart," "Noisy Flushes the Birds," and "Noisy in the Doghouse"—which are, to a fair extent, class comedies. Bob Fraser, the bakery owner, is separated from Noisy Brackett and his wife, members of the country gentry, by the wide gulf of class even more than he recognizes. As one quick indicator of the chasm of class, Bob has twice overheard Sally saying something that he thinks is the name of a horse—"Tray Pays On" ("Noisy in the Doghouse" [*KTMH*, 88])—when Sally is really saying "*tres paysan*," indicating that Bob is very much a peasant. The characters in the Noisy Brackett trilogy are quite heavily but not entirely defined by their class attitudes, and the comedy is fueled by the incongruities that arise from the great differences of attitude and expectation. Social class is also centrally important in "Passing the Ball" (*SS*) and "The Landlord" (*SS*).

Many of Pritchett's stories deal with romantic love and erotic attraction, and his treatment can be comic, ironic, or sincerely emotional. Some of these stories provide a blend of moods and authorial attitudes accomplished by delicate modulations as Pritchett steers the story from one mood to another. The theme of love is sometimes also connected to the theme of self-deception. Love can move a person out of an old life and into a new one, sometimes causing the individual to see a pattern of self-deception in which he or she had been living. But often the treatment will achieve an honest complexity and depth when the author allows the story's form and movement to suggest that the people in love are perhaps trading one set of deceptions for another. Some of the stories that place thematic importance on love or passion are "You Make Your Own Life" (*YMYOL*), "A Spring Morning" (*YMYOL*), "Eleven O'clock" (*YMYOL*), "Blind Love" (*BL*), "The Nest Builder" (*BL*), "The Camberwell Beauty" (*CB*), "The Marvellous Girl" (*CB*), "The Lady from Guatemala" (*CB*), "Did You Invite Me?" (*CB*) "On the Edge of the Cliff" (*OEC*), "The Accompanist" (*OEC*), "The Fig Tree" (*OEC*), "A Family Man" (*OEC*), "The Wedding" (*OEC*), and "A Change of Policy" (*CW*).

The problems and strains of marriage are dealt with humorously, ironically, feelingly, and probingly. "Handsome Is as Handsome Does" (*YMYOL*) is both successful and intriguing because it is a unified story that makes excellent functional use of combined effects. In the three stories of *The Key to My Heart*, which is basically social comedy, a few serious points are nevertheless made about the peculiar psychological ties that bind marriage partners together. Three of the stories from *On the Edge of the Cliff*—"The Accompanist," "The Fig Tree," and "A Family Man"—are sharply observed tales of adultery or betrayal in love. "The Ladder" is both perceptive and humorous. "The Landlord (*SS*) and "Our Wife" (*CB*) are wryly comic but also make telling psychological observations by plays with elements of fantasy.

Pritchett usually introduces his readers rather subliminally to a gray-toned world in which they can feel a pervasive sense of the essential loneliness of his characters. Obviously, Pritchett is not unique in this; in fact, the reason Frank O'Connor titled his study of the short story *The Lonely Voice* is that he felt the genre to be intrinsically well suited for communicating an intense sense of the basic loneliness of the individual—even though he or she may be socially gregarious. In a broader sense the great majority of Pritchett's stories concern loneliness, including certain of the stories listed earlier as love stories. Some of the stories dealing rather centrally with loneliness, though, are "A Careless Widow" (*CW*), "The Sailor" (*IMNH*), "The Spree" (*CB*), "Tea with Mrs. Bittell" (*OEC*), and "A Trip to the Seaside" (*CW*), the last three of which concern loneliness among the elderly.

If Pritchett's stories seem in their content to belong to a world not far removed from the Edwardian, it may be because they provide few direct reflections of the violence that has racked the world for the past three-quarters of a century. "Tea with Mrs. Bittell," with its modest but central representation of urban crime, is an exception. Probably Pritchett feels that the magnitude of the horrors of our time makes them intransigent for treatment in the short story. A few of the stories, however, do deal with war or its aftermath. "The Upright Man" (*YMYOL*) is a parable about how war (in this case World War I), chief instrument of a soulless modern world, chews man up and spits him out. "The Two Brothers" illustrates the destructive effects of the Irish Troubles. "When My Girl Comes Home" and "The Sniff" concern psychological troubles that remain after war is over. One story, "Main Road" (*YMYOL*), a story of social protest, stands virtually alone in Pritchett's fictional canon.

Probably the most atypical of Pritchett's stories are those written in the mode of allegory, parable, or psychological fantasy. These stories—"The Upright Man" (*YMYOL*), "The Scapegoat" (*YMYOL*) "The Ape" (*IMNH*), and "The Citizen" (*WMGCH*)—fall below Pritchett's usual standard. Readers may note, however, that the intriguing "When My Girl Comes Home" (*WMGCH*) gives off the feeling of being a rich, complex, thought-provoking allegory for its time, and that "Tea with Mrs. Bittell," with its suggestions that the title character should be viewed as a desiccated but still feisty Britannia, almost allegorically comments on the diminished state of modern Britain.

Although some of Pritchett's best stories achieve uniqueness partly because of his surefooted but angular—even elliptic—approach, Pritchett has never set out to be an innovator. His caution, practicality, and common sense may be typically English, but they may also be psychological reactions to his father's cloudy romanticism, absurd impracticality, and self-indulgence. Experiments or innovations classifiable by type or readily recognized as such appear seldom in Pritchett's work. A modified stream-of-consciousness technique such as the one he uses in "The Sack of Lights" (*SV*) is mildly effective but unremarkable. Much more rewarding are the narrative and dramatic ironies in "When My Girl Comes Home" (*WMGCH*), "It May Never Happen" (*IMNH*), "The Sailor" (*IMNH*), and (to a lesser extent, because those ironies are, although central, somewhat less complex) those in "Sense of Humour" (*YMYOL*) and "You Make Your Own Life" (*YMYOL*).

Pritchett's Achievement

The resurgence of interest in the short-story form since the 1980s will probably have the effect of directing attention not only to Pritchett's canon but also to his statements about the art of the short story. That Pritchett's own stories provide preeminent examples of the qualities he recommends as essential to the short story is a claim that the modest but assured author would not make. But note how very apt a description of his own work is embodied in a statement he made about the genre: "The short story springs from a spontaneously poetic as distinct from a prosaic impulse—yet is not 'poetical' in the sense of a shuddering sensibility. Because the short story has to be succinct and has to suggest things that have been 'left out,' are, in fact, there all the time, the art calls for a mingling of the skills of the rapid reporter or traveller with an eye for incident and an ear for real speech, the instinct of the poet and ballad-maker, and the sonnet writer's concealed discipline of form" (*OB*, xiv).

Any genuine artist aims at concealed discipline, and the virtue of artlessness is by its nature difficult to demonstrate in an economical way. Pritchett's readers may note, however, that (while it is not all that is implied by "concealed discipline") the best stories do not give the sense of trapping characters and readers inside a machine that will drive them inexorably to a known destination. Pritchett allows his characters at least the illusion of freedom; he appears to respect the selfhood of his characters and the contingent nature of events. Rather like an existentialist, he has said that he is "not very keen on a generalizing morality" and that "the novelist's or the short story writer's duty is to destroy generalization" (Forkner and Séjourné, 30). And the significant accomplishment is that Pritchett can manage to suggest openness, freedom, and contingency while conveying to the reader a firm sense of control—that there is some larger, fully logical, and fully plausible plan discerned only by its creator. Pritchett has an instinct for abetting this sense by his achievement of a tone that manages to seem at once offhand and authoritative. Only an apparent oxymoron like "low-key intensity" can describe the effect of Pritchett's major stories. In writing of short stories generally, John Bayley has observed that "an impression of deadness in the story may arise from too meticulous a control on the part of the writer, and too methodical an awareness of the effects to be achieved."[30] Pritchett long ago issued himself an injunction to avoid such dangers and has consistently abided by it.

Another trademark quality described in Pritchett's comments is the power to suggest what has been "left out." Pritchett works at this: he has said many times that he crafts a short story slowly and meticulously, usually boiling it down from novella length. Selectivity is crucial; creating the aura of suggestion is a delicate art. When something is "left out," readers are usually intrigued enough to try to supply what is missing—to become in a sense cocreators along with the author. When Pritchett writes of how the short story, as opposed to the novel, "wakes the reader up," he means in part that the reader is incited to become an active participant of sorts, rather than loll in the "drugging daydreams" supplied by the novelists.[31] Although Pritchett has a general antipathy to modern critical literary theory, he would probably agree with the now almost universally accepted idea that reader responses to even relatively "open and shut" texts are much more variegated than was once believed. The openness of Pritchett's stories makes reader response even more diverse—so much so, in fact, that modern theorists will deem it doubly anachronistic for Pritchett or anyone else to speak of "the reader," or for me to hazard, even as a convenient shorthand, that "readers are apt" to think something or other. Such stories as "It May Never Happen," "The Sailor," and "Sense of Humour" may well provide fascinating sources for those doing reader-response studies. With the multiplicity of reader responses they appear to invite, these and other stories seem designed to wake readers up.

✦

Pritchett's brand of short story features the open, the implicit, the indeterminate, and the elusive; this strongly dominant tendency accords naturally and well with his largely nonprogrammatic approach to thematic ideas, with his cool ironies and his loving tolerance for the weaknesses of his characters, and with his disinclination for the thrust of ideology into fiction. (If Pritchett was ever really the "embittered left-wing intellectual" [*MO*, 240] a BBC radio producer once saw him as, his fiction scarcely gives any hint of this.) His bent is for the natural, the conversational, and the relaxed; he achieves his frequent heights when he does not strain for effect. Most modern short-story writers accept Pritchett's dictum that "a story must never explain, it must enact and suggest" (Forkner and Séjourné, 27). But a few reviewers, and probably quite a few readers, have deemed it one of Pritchett's serious limitations that he "does not go in for the kill."

What this means, one supposes, is that Pritchett declines to provide strong final effects, dramatic resolutions, or obvious thematic underlinings. One reviewer complained that Pritchett's "aversion for the jugular" is demonstrable because "gestures, not passions, are held as the focus of our attention, and too often we are unsure of what's at stake."[32] Admittedly, Pritchett sometimes carries his techniques of openness and elusiveness a little too far. In most of his stories, however, even the subtle gesture is revelatory of something essentially important; character, setting, and action are suffused, although hardly ever portentously, with symbolic significance. He strives to avoid ideational or thematic overkill; while he is certainly no minimalist, he has a firm sense, both conscious and intuitive, of how "less can be more." Pritchett has acknowledged an important inheritance from Chekhov: "I so much admire Chekhov's stories because they are open-ended, and I try to be as open-ended as possible, leaving things hanging: it's terribly difficult for English writers to do, since some sort of practical or responsible sense works against it" (Haffenden, 219).

✦

To suggest that Pritchett is primarily a symbolist would, of course, be seriously misleading. He is basically a subtle humorist and a revealer of truth through ironies. Occasionally the humor can be broad but complexly textured by the way it functions within a full and sophisticated context. The indelibly comic scene of Hubert Timberlake, the title character of "The Saint," clinging to an overhead branch before sinking slowly into the river is both hilarious and perfectly illustrative of the story's informing idea that it is a constitutive symbol. Other comic scenes are nearly as visually memorable. Readers can imagine the foolishly self-satisfied, barely suppressed grin on the face of Muriel, the Irish girl with "the sense of humour" (in "Sense of Humour") as she rides in the hearse with her new fiancé, gratified to see men tipping their hats in deference to the body of her old boyfriend in the casket right behind her. Other scenes sharply etched in readers' memories can themselves be reminders that comic strands in Pritchett are usually intertwined with serious strands of various kinds. We can laugh at 70-year-old Harry, the protagonist of "On the Edge of the Cliff," as he stands bird-naked, impelled by Eros and egotism, ready to plunge into a cold sea to prove something to himself and his 25-year-old mistress. But the story's deftly modulated tones also cause us to see Harry as a brave fighter against death and decay, an elderly man both sufficiently formidable and admirable. Because Pritchett so often weds plot and character successfully, readers' meditation on the subtleties of incident and gesture often reveal successive layers of character.

One of Pritchett's long-acknowledged strengths is his convincing capture of the real speech of the English, particularly the colloquial language of the lower middle classes. Often some overheard phrase, some single locution or expressed sentiment will give him the basis for a story's comedy. He has remarked, "I have a trained memory for any kind of phrase, anything heard in a shop or in a train" (Forkner and Séjourné, 27). Readers will also note that Pritchett has an unerring ear for the natural rhythms of dialogue, attributable to the good influence of Hemingway. The openings of Pritchett's stories are as accomplished as anyone's; they seem unfussy, sometimes even insouciant, but are always exact and economical in their function. Pritchett quotes Laurence Sterne about not writing until one "hears the tune in one's head" (Forkner and Séjourné, 26). He says that what the writer should really wait for is "to hear the tune of the first sentence and the note you wish to prolong" (Forkner and Séjourné, 26). Relatedly, Pritchett recognizes the achievement of a distinctive voice as crucial for the short story, and most critics agree that few writers have achieved it more consistently than he. And as readers get into a Pritchett story they will often be delighted by fresh metaphors, witty one-liners, and unusual but highly evocative descriptions—in short, imaginative constructs of thought and language that reveal the mind of a poet. Few of these are apt to seem overdone because their very departure from the ordinary or predictably literary only heightens the comic effects, the author's reason for employing them. Pritchett has an impressive arsenal of language at his command, but he uses it in wise moderation. He has hinted several times that much of his own meticulous pruning process involves the cutting away of phrases or sentences he considers overwritten.

❖

The language and technique in any of Pritchett's better stories can be appreciated for their virtuoso effects alone, but they are, of course, subservient to Pritchett's primary purpose—the uncovering of buried or half-buried traits of character. He describes well his own practice:

> A story moves toward a disclosure and that may be an event, a complete revelation of character, the close of a mood, the changing of an emotion, the clinching of an idea, the statement of a situation now completed. . . . [T]he absurdities or the pathos of the private imbroglio has been my story. . . . [T]he story lies in their [his chief characters'] double lives, in the fact that they are themselves story-telling animals, living and yet living by telling a story about

this living at the same time. They dwell—and this to me is the moving and dramatic thing about people—in a solitude which they alone can populate. (*SS*, vi–vii)

Essential to an understanding of Pritchett's characters in general is the idea that each lives in his own solitude but gives himself a feeling of moving out of a spiritual wilderness by telling himself some story—by fabricating some sustaining illusion. Pritchett's implied comments about self-delusion are never anguished but are instead humorous, accepting, and just a bit rueful. In certain of the stories the author, giving the idea of self-delusion ever so slight a turn, suggests that "self-imagination" and "self-invention" may be necessary to the dynamic that allows psychological survival. The pattern Pritchett has most frequently used, with slight variations, throughout his career is to take protagonists seemingly locked away tightly and safely in their ways, subject them to some unforeseen stimulus (frequently that of romantic love or erotic attraction), and watch as their squirming reactions cause the veils of illusion to fall away. Such revelations are generally subtle, though, both for the characters themselves and for readers. It is simply not Pritchett's fictional policy to go in for dramatic underscoring, and it is not part of his nature to engage in loud mocking laughter at either his own characters or real people. And more often than not, the suggestion, implicit but sufficiently clear, is that the foibles of even his eccentric characters are human failings the author has only slightly magnified. Pritchett's compassion is large, very much like Chekhov's, and the artistic alchemy by which he turns the bizarre into the symbolic may have been learned from Dickens.

Pritchett's work is, however, not driven by a particular "philosophy"; he is more interested in people, and even in "things," than in theories. His forte is the rapid capture of a sharply observed set of particular details, so immensely suggestive because so exactly "right" that readers almost immediately feel that they know and believe in the created world. Although hardly ever given full naturalistic description, his locales always have a sense of solidity. Pritchett in fact tells us that it was only when he came to understand just how important a sharp eye can be that he took the first successful steps to being an author. He credits this discovery to advice contained in the 1888 novel of J. M. Barrie (1860–1937), *When a Man's Single*. Although Barrie's novel is both flawed and old-fashioned, it provided advice that breathed life into the young Pritchett's writing career: "The thing to do was to write on the smallest things and those near to you. . . . [T]here is copy in every man you meet [and] when you do meet him you feel inclined to tear it out of him and use it yourself" (*MO*, 29). Although this advice is fairly usual and Pritchett no doubt would soon have met it elsewhere, it is important in that he took it immediately to heart, and ever since has been finding gold in small, out-of-the-way places.

As with many writers, Pritchett did not have to look far to find some of the exact details for his fiction: a number have their genesis in events in which Pritchett himself was either an active participant or a close observer. Among the more successful stories that emerge fairly closely (although, of course, they are artistically transmuted) from Pritchett's own life are "The Diver," "The Sailor," and "The Fly in the Ointment"; others, such as "Sense of Humour" and "The Cage Birds," had their origins in conversational reports (*MO*, 227–28, 22). The several stories involving young clerks all have some basis in their author's own early work experience, including the successful and richly suggestive "It May Never Happen," whose origin is described in *A Cab at the Door*.[33] And readers of the two volumes of autobiography will easily recognize the author's father, Walter Sawdon Pritchett, as the prototype of the irresponsible man of grandiose ideas, the self-deluded, egocentric dreamer and hoarder of "The Fly in the Ointment," "Just a Little More," and "The Lion's Den." It was also Walter Pritchett who brought Christian Science to his son, clearly giving him the impulse for "The Saint," archly and superbly satiric, the funniest of all Pritchett's stories. That "The Saint" also reserves a core of sympathy reveals both Pritchett's skill with complex effects and the ambivalence resulting from its connection with the father he both loved and was appalled by.

Pritchett's two volumes of autobiography, each of which contains its own store of comedy, are also the attempts of a mature man to make sense of his younger self. They provide extremely useful sources of information about the writer. But the second volume, *Midnight Oil*, comes to a hazy conclusion sometime in the mid-1940s (only the last two paragraphs jump ahead to the closing frame of 1970), just after the death of Walter Pritchett, stranding readers in their close knowledge of V. S. Pritchett at midcareer. Pritchett is not like his characters who "keep themselves to themselves" (he is a genial figure familiar to literary men and women as a former president of the English chapter of PEN [1970] and of the international PEN organization [1974]). Still, he is a modest and private person, often reluctant to reveal very much about himself. It is difficult to know what connections may exist between Pritchett's short stories and the events of his life during the past 40 years. His little book *The Turn of the Years: As Old as the Century* (originally published as a magazine essay when he was 80) provides a few snippets of information. He mentions how he still likes to take "ten-mile walks on the cliffs of North Cornwall,"[34] and we can speculate that his walks provided the locales for "On the Edge of the Cliff" and "A Careless Widow." But there is really not much else. It is highly probable but by no means certain that most of the recent stories are a combination of close observation, creative imagination, and memories of past personal events rather than incidents intimately bound up with the writer's personal life.

✦

If there is any "secret" to apprehending the essence of Pritchett's art, it surely resides in understanding how he manages to create and present characters who are both remarkably individuated and clearly representative. Eudora Welty puts it well: "The characters that fill [Pritchett's stories]—erratic, unsure, unsafe, devious, stubborn, restless and desirous, absurd and passionate, all peculiar unto themselves—hold a claim on us that is not to be denied. They demand and get our attention, for in the revelation of their lives, the secrets of our own lives come into view."[35]

Notes to Part 1

1. Anatole Broyard, "On the Edge of the Cliff," *New York Times*, 31 October 1979, sec. 3, p. 27; reprinted in *Books of the Times* (New York: Arno Press, 1979), 2: 538–39.

2. Austin M. Wright, "Recalcitrance in the Short Story," in *Short Story Theory at a Crossroads*, ed. Susan Lohafer and Jo Ellyn Clarey (Baton Rouge: Louisiana State University Press, 1989), 124.

3. Preface to *Collected Stories* (New York: Random House, 1982), x; hereafter cited in text as *CS*.

4. *Midnight Oil* (New York: Random House, 1972), 126; hereafter cited in text as *MO*.

5. Dean R. Baldwin, *V. S. Pritchett* (Boston: Twayne, 1987), 61; hereafter cited in text.

6. Paul Binding, "A Kindly Art" (review of *The Complete Short Stories*), *New Statesman and Society*, 23 November 1990, 38.

7. John Haffenden, "V. S. Pritchett," *Novelists in Interview* (London: Methuen, 1985), 223; hereafter cited in text.

8. William Peden, "V. S. Pritchett," in *The English Short Story: 1880–1945*, ed. Joseph M. Flora (Boston: Twayne, 1985), 146.

9. William Peden, "Realism and Anti-realism," in *The Teller and the Tale: Aspects of the Short Story*," ed. Wendell M. Aycock (Lubbock: Texas Tech Press, 1982), 61.

10. Douglas A. Hughes, "V. S. Pritchett: An Interview," *Studies in Short Fiction* 13 (Fall 1976): 429; hereafter cited in text.

11. John Vickery and J'nan M. Sellery, "Ritual in the Streets: A Study of Pritchett's 'The Scapegoat,'" in *Ritual and Literature*, ed. Vickery and Sellery (Boston: Houghton and Mifflin, 1972), 236; hereafter cited in text.

12. Preface to *The Sailor, Sense of Humour, and Other Stories* (New York: Alfred A. Knopf, 1956), vii; hereafter cited in text as *SS*.

13. Shusha Guppy and Anthony Weller, "The Art of Fiction CXXII: V. S. Pritchett," *Paris Review* 117 (Winter 1990): 201; hereafter cited in text.

14. Ben Forkner and Philippe Séjourné, "An Interview with V. S. Pritchett," *Journal of the Short Story in English* 6 (Spring 1986): 24; hereafter cited in text.

15. Geneviève Doze, "Two Tentative Readings of 'Many Are Disappointed,' by V. S. Pritchett," *Journal of the Short Story in English* 6 (Spring 1986): 64.

16. Introduction to *The Oxford Book of Short Stories*, chosen by V. S. Pritchett (New York: Oxford University Press, 1981), xiv; hereafter cited in text as *OB*.

17. Robert W. Smith, "Visiting with Sir Victor," *Washington Post Book World*, 18 November 1979, 8.

18. "The Writer's Tale," *Vogue* 17 (March 1981): 362; hereafter cited in text as

"WT."

19. "The Short Story," *London Magazine* 6 (September 1966): 61; hereafter cited in text as "TSS."

20. Robertson Davies, "V. S. Pritchett: Storyteller Supreme" (review of *Collected Stories*), *Washington Post Book World*, 25 April 1982, 2.

21. "The Temptations of a Technique," *Times Literary Supplement*, 6 October 1961, 657.

22. Susan Lohafer, "'The Wheelbarrow' by V. S. Pritchett," in her *Coming to Terms with the Short Story* (Baton Rouge: Louisiana State University Press, 1983), 151; hereafter cited in text.

23. Quoted by Michael Williams, "Welsh Voices in the Short Story," in *Little Reviews Anthology: 1949*, ed. Denys Val Baker (London: Methuen, 1949), 103.

24. William Peden, *"Blind Love and Other Stories,"* *Saturday Review*, 14 March 1970, 38.

25. *London Perceived* (San Diego: Harcourt Brace, n.d.), 41.

26. Anatole Broyard, "Ah, Sweet Mystery of Life" (review of *The Camberwell Beauty*), *New York Times*, 16 September 1974, 33.

27. Cécile Oumhani, "Water in V. S. Pritchett's Art of Revealing," *Journal of the Short Story in English* 6 (Spring 1986): 76.

28. Pascal Aquien, "'The Diver' or the Plunge into Fantasy," *Journal of the Short Story in English* 6 (Spring 1986): 51.

29. In this chapter I use the following abbreviations for the story collections cited: *BL* (*Blind Love and Other Stories*); *CB* (*The Camberwell Beauty and Other Stories*); *CW* (*A Careless Widow and Other Stories*); *IMNH* (*It May Never Happen and Other Stories*); *KTMH* (*The Key to My Heart*); *OEC* (*On the Edge of the Cliff and Other Stories*); *SS* (*The Sailor, Sense of Humour, and Other Stories*); *SV* (*The Spanish Virgin and Other Stories*); *WMGCH* (*When My Girl Comes Home*); *YMYOL* (*You Make Your Own Life*).

30. John Bayley, *The Short Story* (New York: St. Martin's, 1988), 35.

31. "Short Stories," in *What Is the Short Story?*, rev. ed., ed. Eugene Current-Garcia and Walton R. Patrick (Glenview, Illinois: Scott, Foresman, 1974), 117.

32. Jonathan Penner, "Glimpses of Illicit Love" (review of *On the Edge of the Cliff*), *Washington Post Book World*, 18 December 1979, 9.

33. See *A Cab at the Door* (London: Chatto & Windus, 1968), 230–33.

34. *The Turn of the Years: As Old as the Century* (New York: Random House, 1982), 34.

35. Eudora Welty, "A Family of Emotions" (review of *Selected Stories*), *New York Times Book Review*, 25 June 1978, 1.

Part 2

THE WRITER

Introduction

Although the exposure of puritanism is a repeated theme in Pritchett's work, one vestige of a puritan heritage remains in the man himself: his work ethic was still severe when he was 90. Not only a fiction writer, Pritchett is still busy as a literary journalist of the first order (rivaled in England perhaps only by Anthony Burgess). While characteristically genial, he has felt he has had little time for interviews, and has granted relatively few. In *The Turn of the Years* he comments on one of the ways in which his wife, Dorothy, provides invaluable assistance: "It is she who charms away the swarms of people who telephone, the speculators who think I exist for reading their theses and books, for more and more reviews, for giving interviews or lectures or signing their applications for grants."[1]

The interview conducted by Douglas Hughes focuses sharply on the short fiction. In this interview as elsewhere, Pritchett comes across as modest (but not self-deprecatory), straightforward, and unpretentious. He appears to value balance and good sense in interviews as much as he does in his criticism; he has a disinclination for heavy theory and self-important generalizations. Unlike many self-taught men, he is comfortable enough within himself to wear his learning easily.

In his essay "The Writer's Tale" Pritchett offers a succinct commentary on the art and recent history of the short story; his qualities of charm, honesty, and seemingly effortless perspicacity are again in evidence.

Note

1. *The Turn of the Years* (Wilton, U.K.: Michael Russell, 1981), 35.

Interview, 1975

Douglas A. Hughes

V. S. Pritchett has been a distinguished British man of letters for five decades. He has written several novels, volumes of literary criticism, travel books, a highly praised autobiography (*A Cab at the Door* and *Midnight Oil*) and he has been an editor of the *New Statesman*. In his seventy-sixth year he continues to review books for the *New Yorker* and the *New York Review of Books*. But Mr. Pritchett's first love has been the short story, in which he has excelled. I do not believe it would be an exaggeration to claim that he is one of the best British story writers in this century. He has written eight volumes of stories, the latest being *The Camberwell Beauty and Other Stories* (1974). In 1975 he was knighted for his "service to literature."

Mr. Pritchett, who in May was presiding over a P.E.N. conference in Paris when I arrived in London, generously agreed to meet with me as soon as he returned to England. This interview was conducted in the living room of Mr. Pritchett's London apartment not far from Regents Park on May 27, 1975.

✦

INTERVIEWER: For many years you've been a successful writer with the short story, novel, literary criticism, and travel books. In the Preface to *The Sailor, Sense of Humour and Other Stories* you've written that the short story is the only form of writing that has given you great pleasure. You say that despite difficulties of the form itself, you've found that the short story has stimulated you. I'd like you to talk briefly about the pleasures of writing the short story as opposed to other forms of literature.

PRITCHETT: I think the short story has a certain amount of mixed excitement, that is to say, the excitement the poet feels when he has his image or his starting in his mind and watches it grow. It also has that almost sensational quality that the reporter feels when he sees something happen and then reports it exactly. The curious combination of the reporter and the poet in the short story writer is a strange combination but I believe it exists.

"V. S. Pritchett: An Interview," *Studies in Short Fiction* 13 (Fall 1976): 423–32. © 1976 by Newberry College. Reprinted by permission.

The other thing is that the short story is delightful because it is very much like looking at a picture. You can see the whole picture at once. A story is a thing which can be seen at once. You can't see *War and Peace, Middlemarch*, any long novel at once. Furthermore, the story has intensity in it. It's the intensity, I think, that attracts me.

INTERVIEWER: You've suggested that the short story is a particularly apt form for our time "overwhelmed by enormous experience." You wrote in 1956 that we'd rather "glance at experience than look at it full in the face." Now, do you think that this remark still holds true for today, 1975?

PRITCHETT: I think it does. Nowadays the situation in which almost any of us lives in relation to society is becoming more and more complex and frightening. For instance, we may have to deal with terrorism and we certainly didn't before. We also have had to deal with human relationships in new ways. People may be ill and go to psychiatrists, to which people didn't go before. There are economic, interracial, and other difficulties that present themselves as frightful problems to the ordinary man. It requires an immense saturation in these subjects in order to be able to achieve some sort of detachment from them, which is necessary when you come to writing. You can't write, so to speak, from the middle of the storm, or not easily. So the short story, with its glancing view, can contain a great deal, can pay attention to aspects of these problems, which are very important, but it needn't state the whole of them. One of the advantages of the short story is that it allows us to isolate certain things in present day life.

INTERVIEWER: How do you explain, or don't you think about, the critical neglect of the genre itself? Isn't it curious that the short story is not taken very seriously by critics?

PRITCHETT: Well, I think that is partially due to the general decline in the short story owing to the disappearance of periodicals. All the great short-story writers had periodicals which would publish them. The people loved reading stories. In a sense they had little else to do. They didn't have a television to look at, a motor car to drive, a swimming pool to swim in. They couldn't travel easily from one place to another. Therefore they read and one of their favorite forms of reading was the story. There were plenty of periodicals of very high quality. The evening newspaper had stories of very high quality, not just popular stuff.

INTERVIEWER: I was just thinking that Maupassant's stories appeared in newspapers.

PRITCHETT: Maupassant's stories appeared in newspapers. So did Chekhov's and Poe's stories. That kind of thing has vanished. There followed then the magazines and little reviews. They have slowly ebbed away. The result has been that the public has lost this literary form that it used to enjoy. Secondly, I think short-story writers have always been rather few and far between. The number of first class short-story writers in any country has been very few compared with the number of novelists, shall we say. It simply is because the short story is a particularly difficult and special kind of art.

INTERVIEWER: Let me interrupt for a second. There's one thing. If you take recent quality writers of the British short story: H. E. Bates, Sean O'Faolain, Frank O'Connor, Mary Lavin, and yourself. Let's take only those, all right? There's very little critical commentary on these writers considering their achievement. What I can't understand is why there should be 275 articles written next year on James Joyce and the works of these story writers should be almost totally ignored. That's what I'm getting at.

PRITCHETT: I know. It's very extraordinary, isn't it?

INTERVIEWER: I think of the short story as the Neglected Genre.

PRITCHETT: In fact, there are very few books on the short story. Frank O'Connor wrote one. So did Sean O'Faolain.

INTERVIEWER: H. E. Bates wrote one, though it is a historical survey.

PRITCHETT: Oh, yes, so he did. The short story is a subject that has been entirely neglected.

INTERVIEWER: How do you explain that?

PRITCHETT: It may be somehow the short story speaks for itself.

INTERVIEWER: Do you really believe that? Isn't a short story much like a lyric poem?

PRITCHETT: Yes, yes , it is.

INTERVIEWER: In many cases a story is very complicated and subtle and there are a lot of things that one can say about it.

PRITCHETT: Nobody does it, I must say. In fact, if you take the case of Turgenev, who wrote both short stories and novels—his stories differ very much from his novels. In any book on Turgenev the critic gives a brief chapter on his short stories, which contain some of his best work, and there are hundreds of pages about his novels.

INTERVIEWER: All right, is it possible that we might conclude that critics or people generally really undervalue the story, and I particularly address this question to you because somewhere you've said that the short story is a minor art. Why would you depreciate it and consider it a minor art any more than a collection of lyric poems would be considered minor art?

PRITCHETT: When I said that I was being rather ironical because there was a period, which I think came to an end about ten years ago, when there was a very strong feeling that the short story was done for. The reason it was supposedly done for was that it's rather like the sonnet. It's a very complicated form of writing and it requires a certain skill. You can't compare a sonnet with *Paradise Lost* and you shouldn't do so. But on the other hand people do, in the back of their minds, say, oh it's short and therefore it must be much more important to write something long rather than a story. And that's what it amounts to.

INTERVIEWER: That's exactly how I feel about it. It's so easy to depreciate the short story. I didn't realize you were being ironic in your remark.

PRITCHETT: I was being rather modest about it in order to make a dig. My statement was immediately denied by others when I wrote it. But people also did say that it was an inferior form of writing because it was essentially a craft. They were thinking, for example, of the immense amount of craftsmanlike ingenuity which Kipling used, especially in his later stories, which were very elaborate. Or they were thinking of a Russian writer like Babel, who, to write a story of fifteen pages, would perhaps write a hundred and fifty pages and then reduce it, reduce it, reduce it. That's obviously a matter not of vision but of craftsmanship that has frequently been brought against short-story writers, that they are essentially craftsmen. I don't think it's true.

INTERVIEWER: It may be true of some story writers. I think one could only be a craftsman and write readable stories, but it wouldn't be true of the best writers certainly.

PRITCHETT: It's not true, not at all. Another great thing about the short story is that the writer, the good one, always has a voice you can instantly recognize. You only have to read the first three lines and you can pretty well tell who wrote it. The actual pitch of his voice tells you straightaway. In a novelist this isn't necessarily so. It's very difficult to take test passages say from Dickens or George Eliot or Hardy. It's by no means certain that you'll recognize that distinct voice. The novelist is relying on the general public voice, no doubt of an educated kind, but nevertheless a general voice that everyone uses and understands. But the short-story writer is like someone who sings a song. The singer has his own voice. It isn't the voice of anyone else.

INTERVIEWER: Did you ever consider writing a book of criticism on the short story?

PRITCHETT: No, never. I have written short critical articles about certain writers that I've admired. No, I think it's much better to write another story rather than write a book about short stories.

INTERVIEWER: What do you think of Frank O'Connor as a critic of the short story?

PRITCHETT: I think he's extremely interesting about it because he had one particularly interesting theory, that the story was especially suited to anarchic societies. There were anarchic societies in Russia, America, and Ireland and there the short story flourished. In England, no, and therefore among English writers there was a long silence through the nineteenth century as far as the short story was concerned.

INTERVIEWER: He also said that the short story deals with a submerged group, with the outsider. Do you think that this is true?

PRITCHETT: I suppose to some extent this is true. You don't feel, however, that Chekhov or Turgenev was an outsider. I think he may be right in saying that stories deal with the submerged part of the self, which is quite another matter. If you take the most conventional character you can think of, the most complete insider shall we say, and you write a story about him you are almost certain to choose the part of his person that is submerged or hidden. You're not likely to write about the surface, otherwise you'd become a photographer. I don't think that the short-story writer is a photographer at all. Everyone feels himself to be exceptional and the writer tends to look at that part of the human being that is submerged, that separates the individual from others of his own kind.

INTERVIEWER: In an introduction to the collected stories of Mary Lavin you made an interesting observation. You said that the Russians, Italians, the Slavonic Jews, and the Irish excel at the short story. I'm curious why you left out the Americans. It seems to me that the Americans have succeeded marvelously with the short story.

PRITCHETT: Absolutely. I don't know why I left them out. I entirely agree with you.

INTERVIEWER: In your autobiography you say that you object to the contention that you create characters in the Dickensian sense in your stories. Perhaps this is true, but to an American reader your fiction has an unmistakable British quality. You go on to say that far from being a traditional English writer there is a foreign element in your work. What do you mean by this foreign element?

PRITCHETT: Well, this theory about myself may be quite wrong but I felt myself not to be terribly interested in English life when I was young, before I went to live abroad. I spent six or seven years abroad between the ages of twenty and about twenty-seven. I had, as young men do, certain vanities in being rather foreign to my own environment. When I was in France I liked to feel myself a Frenchman and while in Spain to feel myself a Spaniard and hoped that some of this would rub off on me. This is partly the reason. And then as I got to know many writers that I admired, I realized that they had the same sort of feeling that they didn't quite belong to the community in which they lived. We were therefore people who had the feeling of living on a frontier between two possibilities. I think—I don't quite know how to put this—I think really it is the frontier spirit which I had very strongly felt and still do feel very much. About being Dickensian, many people say that about my writing and I certainly don't object to it because it's an enormous compliment. But on the other hand Dickens was a very great writer who was sort of centrally English in all of his comic characters. You've only got to go out and down the street to meet them in two minutes. And they don't know they're being what they are. But Dickens saw and very deeply felt that what was happening to English people in his time was that they were working too hard, that the doctrine of work in the nineteenth century was just killing them. It was killing their souls, but they had this ability to construct a fantasy life which they gradually assumed to be real. He did everything he could to encourage the flourishing of this fantasy life. The best example I can think of is the alteration he made to an article that someone had written about the postal system for the paper he edited, *Household Words.* He had an article written on how the post office was organized and how you posted letters and what happened to them and so on. The writer had described the frantic scene at the post office at six o'clock in the evening when you had to get your mail posted in order to get it through at a cheap rate. At that hour you couldn't get into a post office because of the crowds pushing and shoving and even throwing their papers over the crowds to the counter. Dickens understood that the original writer was a rather dull fellow who described this scene. Dickens, in his alteration, began to exaggerate everything in the scene and finally described at the end how someone decided to throw the office boy clean across the crowd. Now this idea of throwing the office boy on to the counter is a fantasy, but I'm sure many people in the crowd at that time thought: it's a pity we can't throw this boy across. This was a release. If he could see these exceptional fantasies that entered the imaginations of ordinary people, Dickens thought he could make them grow. He would be describing something that would be profoundly true of the English character. Well, I feel equally when I see someone who appears prosaic but who after I've got to know him suddenly reveals things about himself that are absolutely incredible. . . . I realize that the incredible is part of his real character. Well, in the sense that I focus on this incredible element sometimes I may be Dickensian but not in the sense of just going in for funny people. For most of the people I've written fantastic things about are not funny people at all.

INTERVIEWER: You've said that every short story is a drama and for you the drama lies in the human personality. I think I understand what you mean by this, but I wonder why you emphasize character at the expense of events or situations. Wouldn't you agree that situations, particularly unusual situations, play a very important part in most of your stories?

PRITCHETT: Yes they do, indeed. That's quite true. I think many writers, before they get down to the unusual situations, have one or two characters in mind. And sometimes these characters grow larger and larger of themselves and become, as it were, like stories. In others they are put in extraordinary situations and in fact their very characters attract unusual situations to them.

INTERVIEWER: In revealing character you appear to be working throughout the story rather than in the Joycean manner of epiphany. Would you agree?

PRITCHETT: Yes, I think on the whole I would, yes.

INTERVIEWER: And the next question is: you've said that when *Ulysses* was published you were living in Paris but you didn't read the novel until several years later. Did you read *Dubliners* early, when it first appeared?

PRITCHETT: I read *Dubliners* very early.

INTERVIEWER: Did those stories make an impression on you? Did they influence you?

PRITCHETT: I was very much influenced by Irish stories. In fact, I only began writing short stories when I went to Ireland [as a journalist] and found there were several interesting story writers there. I didn't know them, of course, but I knew their work. Joyce, of course, was one and Liam O'Flaherty was writing at that time. Sean O'Faolain may have written later. I suddenly recognized their curious poetic gift, if you understand poetic in the sense of a sensation, was very much an Irish gift and it did appeal to me enormously. The danger was that I should think of the Irish, as one often does, as just being funny because they say funny things. One had to grow out of that sort of thing and get at the real essence of what they were trying to say.

INTERVIEWER: In commenting on the stories of Mary Lavin you've said that Irish storytellers tend to concentrate on the discrepancy between ordinary, everyday life and the self's hidden life. Isn't this in fact your own approach to characterization, a disclosing of the duality of the individual?

PRITCHETT: It is very much so, yes. I never see people as being consistent with themselves at all.

INTERVIEWER: Most of your characters live in a world of self-deception. Isn't that essentially what you're showing, that these characters are living in an illusion?

PRITCHETT: They're living partly in their imaginations. And after all, I think people. . . . There's something I call self-imagination. We are what we are, but we often imagine ourselves as something else and it's that which I'm considering.

INTERVIEWER: Then yours is a consistently ironic tone.

PRITCHETT: Yes, that is true.

INTERVIEWER: Would it be fair to assume that your vision of life is that man lives in illusion?

PRITCHETT: Yes, certainly.

INTERVIEWER: Would you accept the judgment that your work indicates that man's collective lot is one of failure and unhappiness?

PRITCHETT: Well, I think we live like tightrope walkers walking over a Niagara. Fortunately, we have enough—what should I say?—cussedness to survive the walk with some sort of balance.

INTERVIEWER: It appears that your comic characters become grotesques—at least what might be considered grotesques—by dedicating themselves too unreservedly to their own personal views of reality, one which is cut off from conventional reality or truth. You talk about the essence of comedy as being "militancy." That's your word. Is militancy another word for fanaticism or the spirit of the seriousness that Nietzsche speaks of?

PRITCHETT: No, I don't mean it in that sense. In comedy, I think, there's a general fight for survival that goes on. Almost every character feels himself entirely alone, and therefore he's engaged in a battle of wits with his purely imaginary enemies. I think this is very common in Jane Austen, a very militant writer in that sense.

INTERVIEWER: Do you think that literature has a purpose, a function to serve? I ask this question knowing that in your whole literary career you've been very independent from ideological and philosophical positions, that you've been a very self-effacing writer. But do you see literature as having a function to serve in society?

PRITCHETT: It's kind of a secret means of communication between people. Literature enlarges our knowledge and possibilities of human nature to an extraordinary degree. It makes us aware of people, emotions, and ideas of which we are normally unaware or which we take for granted. It's really a secret communication.

INTERVIEWER: Then you regard the writer more as an observer in the manner of Flaubert and Joyce than as a mover in the manner of Tolstoy and Dostoevsky?

PRITCHETT: I'm not a didactic writer. I really think that the writer is an observer, a recorder of human experience. But he himself may be observing in extreme difficulty; that is to say, he may be in the middle of something which he can't always clearly observe.

INTERVIEWER: In your autobiography you mention the early influence on your writing: Stevenson, Chesterton, Anatole France. What about later influences? Was Hemingway an influence in his use of language?

PRITCHETT: Very much so, yes. When I wrote "Sense of Humour" it was very much under the influence of Hemingway, although it may not seem so to the reader. That was a story I had been trying to write for six or seven years. I had written various versions of it. I thought it wasn't any good and I set it aside. Then suddenly reading Hemingway I thought: my god, yes, I believe I can write it, and then I threw away my other versions and wrote it in a particular way.

INTERVIEWER: Was "Many Are Disappointed" written at the same time?

PRITCHETT: Approximately the same time.

INTERVIEWER: Because that story seems to me to clearly show Hemingway's influence in the language and tone.

PRITCHETT: Probably. He possibly had some influence, though I don't remember that quite so much. Yes, it must come under that. Certainly the thing people say I'm quite good at is writing dialogue, knowing how different kinds of people speak. Hemingway knew that and I, who never met any of those characters in the story "Many Are Disappointed," suddenly realized how four men, going on a biking tour like that, would speak to each other. The background of the story is simply that I was once down in Cornwall and was bicycling or walking along and wanted a drink. I came to such a place as found in the story and there was the same kind of woman serving tea. I thought that it was very disappointing and went on. Afterward I thought how splendid it would be to have four men going along, each with his own particular fantasy or expectation, arriving at such a place. And that's how it grew.

INTERVIEWER: Now that brings up another question. How your stories come about, how they're actually conceived and written. In reading about your life I get the feeling that a number of your stories have an autobiographical background.

PRITCHETT: That is so, yes.

INTERVIEWER: But do you write some stories that are totally outside your experience, stories which are pure imagination?

PRITCHETT: I do. [Pause] I'm just trying to remember my stories.

INTERVIEWER: There's one story I'm particularly fond of, "Blind Love."

PRITCHETT: That's totally outside my experience. The origin of that story was that I was told of a blind man who went to a faith healer.

INTERVIEWER: It's a great story. Are you especially fond of it or is it just another story to you?

PRITCHETT: No. I think it's a good story, but it's not part of my experience.

INTERVIEWER: Do you keep a notebook for your stories?

PRITCHETT: Yes, I do.

INTERVIEWER: What I'm getting at here is how you actually go about writing stories. You have a notebook. Do you work every day on a story? Do you work when it moves you or when you get an idea? How do you work and how do the stories come about?

PRITCHETT: Well, I do, from time to time, make notes of things. All sorts of unusual things, like people speaking in the streets. Situations sometimes and sometimes I'll make a note of a particular feeling. And then sometimes from real life some incident occurs or some people I know will say something and I'll write it down. I think that if I make a list of these things they may stir some sort of story in me. But the story that results from such notes is *never* the story that is related to the people or events of real life. I get a lot of ideas for stories, but I find that I make false starts so I generally try to write three stories at the same time. If I write one I get stuck. Then I'll move on to the next one and I'll get stuck with that one. Then I move on to the next one and then I go back to the first one and continue.

INTERVIEWER: In *Midnight Oil* you say that the cost of literature is higher than most readers imagine and is getting higher. What did you mean by that?

PRITCHETT: [Pause] I'm not really sure in what sense I meant that. But I must say I find the act of writing much more exacting now than I did when I was starting out, that is, after I had learned how to write. I believe writers continue to write well so long as they make difficulties for themselves. If you arrive at a certain point of success where you no longer have difficulties then your growth ceases. Your writing becomes easier and not so exacting and then you begin to go down hill. You become less interesting. So I think it is the concentration on difficulty which is important to writers. And actually the more experience you have the more exacting you become because you choose more obstacles.

INTERVIEWER: Speaking of literary success, I recently came across a remark by W. H. Auden I'd like you to comment on. Auden wrote in the Introduction to Paul Valéry's *Analects:* "Aside from the money, literary success can give but small satisfaction to an author, even to his vanity. For what does literary success mean? To be condemned by persons who have not read his works and to be imitated by persons devoid of talent. There are two kinds of literary glory that are worth winning but the writer who wins either will never know. One is to have been the writer, perhaps a quite minor one, in whose work some great master generations later finds an essential clue for solving some problem; the other is to become for someone else an example of the dedicated life, 'being secretly invoked, pictured, and placed by a stranger in an inner sanctum of his thoughts, so as to serve him as a witness, a judge, a father, and a hallowed mentor.'"

PRITCHETT: I think that's a rather good statement. The great moment in a writer's life is having the excitement of his initial idea, the moment when a sudden vision comes: good heavens. I can do this. And then comes the appalling labor of trying to do it, when the writer may become increasingly disappointed and finally lose all self-confidence. And then the whole thing is over because he's finished and it's left him with almost nothing. He's got to go on to the next thing. However, it is an enormous comfort to a writer and one of the great rewards of writing to find that what you've written has meant something to another writer or writers or to other people and that you're part of the continuity of literature. Of course, your quality as a writer is your own personal business, which you really want to perfect. You want to perfect yourself and that sort of self-perfection is its own reward. But I think that *every* writer is valuable insofar as he helps other writers. Last night, for example, I happened to pick up by accident Gibbon's *Decline and Fall of the Roman Empire* and read two or three pages. I'm not an historian and don't know anything about the Roman Empire; nevertheless, a few sentences there absolutely stuck in my mind. And I thought: thank God for Gibbon. You see, that started my mind working and so I'm grateful for Gibbon.

"The Writer's Tale"

The writing of short stories has been a fate with me since I was very young, when I could not stop listening to my mother's tales, and telling my own. I have written five novels, but the short story is the only form of writing that elates me, perhaps because it is difficult.

It has not in the least dismayed me to hear people say in the last forty years that "no one reads short stories," or "what we want to know is what happened afterwards." Despite the decline in the number of periodicals on which the story to some extent depends for a living, we story writers can rely on a body of addicted readers, partly because they can turn our phrases over and over again on their tongues, partly because ours is a *memorable* art. Whereas one forgets large tracts of even the greatest novels, the short story sticks in our minds for years, very much in the same way a painting remains vividly in the mind and becomes richer the more one looks at it. It does not surprise me when I hear publishers and booksellers say now that "no one wants long works of fiction," and that public taste is turning to shorter works. We do not want the lump of rock; we want the diamond. Because it crystallizes, the short story seems to be the natural form of fiction, most natural to the way most of us live now. People used to speak of the pleasure of "losing" themselves in the novel; present-day readers, in our threatened century, turn to the story in order to have the uncommon experience of "finding themselves" in a specific and not diffused experience.

We are not as solidly at ease as we were in the heyday of the novel. We are alert to our dissatisfactions. We live in a nervous, restless age, ourselves fragmented as we glance at one another. There is no longer a prolonged steady gaze. We are forced to see our own and other people's lives in side glances; we ask for the essence, not the paragraph. Living, as we do, in mass society in which we are asked to be anonymous, we look for the moment in which our privacy breaks through and reveals its significance in our comedies and disasters. In that moment people become publicly mem-

"The Writer's Tale" by V. S. Pritchett, *Vogue*, March 1981, 327–28, 362. © 1981 by V. S. Pritchett. Reprinted by permission of Sterling Lord Literistic, Inc.

orable for their own private sake. The moment may be gentle, violent, ridiculous or passionate—one remembers Kipling's terrifying "Mary Postgate," or the dumb response of the captured soldiers in Frank O'Connor's "Guests of the Nation," or the feet of the Borstal boy awakening his mind in Alan Sillitoe's "The Loneliness of the Long-Distance Runner."

It is clear that the craft of the short-story writer is very different from the ruminating craft of the novelist. Neither Kipling nor Chekhov, both of them masters, could write novels; to my mind, D. H. Lawrence's novels are inferior to his stories. The story has to construct a form that drives home what is to be said. It has to be succinct and piercing. It has to leave out in order to put something sharper and more telling in. Novelists can cover up faults of design; the short story cannot. The writer has to contrive a mode that calls for a mingling of the skills of the rapid reporter with a quick eye and ear for speech, the instincts of the poet or ballad-maker—for the echoes and shadows of the outside world must be evoked in the tale. He has to cultivate the moralist's gift for aphorism and wit. I fear the word "poet" may give the casual reader the false impression that one has to be "poetical." One does not. I would say that P. G. Wodehouse was a poet in his comedies—comedy being an inverted poetry. As in contemporary poets like Fuller, Enright, and Larkin, the "poetic" lies in the terse arrangement of laconic spoken phrases that discloses the stretches of complex feeling that lie between the lines. A short story is an evocation, a work of disclosure and in this—when you reread it, as you will—it is like a tale of detection and has to be written with the same care for ingenious construction. Above all, the short-story writer must have a distinctive voice and that sense of design; once again, in our society, what we long for is a sense of shape in our lives, the recognition that our emotions have an architecture which distinguishes us from others.

I was certainly influenced by Dickens a little when I was young because I am interested in the way people project their fantastic self-imagination; by Irish writers like O'Connor and Liam O'Flaherty; by Russians who were not bound by clock time and arbitrary plots and by their "strange" sense of the lost hours of the day; by Hemingway's use of real rather than novelised speech—people rarely answer one another in ordinary talk and have a "poetic" delight in repetition: it makes them important. Yet no one can possibly resemble the writers who influence him. The short-story writer has to master the art of leaving out; he invents imaginary selves. A casual overhead phrase—"I keep myself to myself"—started me writing "Sailor." A flutter of tiny waves on a quiet sea started me thinking of "On the Edge of the Cliff." One carries around with one a huge collection of unoccupied characters who beg to become stories and to be justified. The sight of a woman catching a flea in a pub was the beginning of "Things as They Are."

Kipling, D. H. Lawrence, and Conrad seem to me the finest of English short-story writers, and George Moore's "Celibates" absurdly neglected. It must be remembered that after Sir Walter Scott's "The Two Drovers," the immense influence of the great English novelists in the nineteenth century often turned the short story into what looks like the discarded chapter of a novel and that, consequently, in Great Britain we had a much later start than the Americans who had fewer novelists. They also benefited by belonging to a society more open than our own. They had a classless vernacular which came to us late, and a native interest in cunning, exaggeration and fable; they knew that everything depends on the opening sentence which sets the tone and not—except in O. Henry, as in Maupassant—in the payoff.

In my generation, stories like H. E. Bates's "The Mill" and many of Elizabeth Bowen's break new ground. In "Fireman Flower" William Sansom showed we had ornate fantasies of our own. We have been strong in travelers—Stevenson and Maugham, a master in Conrad, and continuing the tradition of "abroad" we now have Nadine Gordimer, Doris Lessing, the brisk and witty Paul Theroux (an American-Londoner) and Mavis Gallant, Frank Tuohy, Olivia Manning and V. S. Naipaul with their searching evocation of post-war foreign exile, and the fatalistic yet robust India of Ruth Prawer Jhabvala. The gifts of writers like Elspeth Davie, Susan Hill, Muriel Spark, and Edna O'Brien speak with the language of the times. I find William Trevor outstanding, particularly in a terrifying Irish story like "Attracta"—in which we see the effects of the memory of old violence. He moves to a subtle or to an arresting moral change in his people. And in young Mr. McEwan we have an original explorer of the scenes of seedy porn and adolescent delinquency who has a remarkable command of styles and design. I could mention many others, much younger than myself, whose talents show that what has been called "the modest art" is vigorously original as it explores what goes on in their generation. Our strange British deficiency is the disappearance of our humorists. For that, I suppose, we must blame contemporary deadpan anxiety but I do not think we should use that as an excuse for not being robust in the laughing imagination. In America, the occasional short writings of Saul Bellow have it. We once had it. Our times are not short of congenial, posturing hypocrites, con-men and enduring fools.

Part 3

THE CRITICS

Introduction

To a large extent V. S. Pritchett is a writer's writer—an artist greatly admired by other professionals who work in the field of short fiction. Since the mid-1940s practitioners of the short-story form who read Pritchett have been able to look with admiration at a level of craftsmanship that makes the product of numerous revisions seem the effortless creation of a few moments. I have selected essays by Eudora Welty and William Trevor not simply because they are other preeminent short fictionists providing warm accolades, but also because they provide sensitive and beautifully articulated insights into Pritchett's artistry. Although their sentiments might not be so eloquently expressed, numerous other major writers hold Pritchett in an esteem nearly as high as that in which he is held by Welty and Trevor.

Pritchett has always had a number of dedicated general readers too, and many new ones have discovered him as a result of the prominently situated reviews of the various volumes of collected stories. But the relative neglect of the short-story form, combined with the subtle textures and elusive meanings of Pritchett's stories, have until recently caused him to be virtually ignored in the academy, except for an occasional bowing acknowledgment or favorable nod; not one of his short fictions has been the object of a sustained analysis or developed commentary. Writing as recently as 1982, Douglas A. Hughes was able to point correctly to this lamentable disregard in a guest editorial in the journal *Studies in Short Fiction*. I am gratified Professor Hughes has agreed to provide for this section an illuminating original essay on a recurrent theme in Pritchett's later short fiction.

Douglas A. Hughes

For most of his half-century-long career as a short-story writer, V. S. Pritchett has been giving narrative form to the comic spirit in a way that distinguishes him from most of his contemporaries. In fact, it is the robust, wholesome quality of his comic vision that helps to engender the peculiar feelings of warmth and confidence readers typically experience with his stories. Unlike most other writers of serious comedy, Pritchett avoids censuring the modern world or disparaging his characters when they are weak or foolish. It is curious that even those writers who deliberately try to steer clear of satire often become so exasperated with the frailties and follies of their characters that they lose patience with them and yield to the temptation of ridiculing these all-too-human beings, thus invoking the spirit of satire despite themselves. This is decidedly not Pritchett's way.

He, like James Joyce—however different the two writers appear in other respects—possesses a comic vision that is patently celebratory. Although it may appear gratuitous to associate Pritchett with Joyce, few other writers in this century so consistently celebrate the joy of life in the midst of frustration, loss, and loneliness. Pritchett unconditionally accepts both the messy real world and his flawed characters as they are without denying the absurdity of either. Like Joyce, he demonstrates what has been termed "comic faith: a tacit belief that the world is both funny and potentially good; a pattern of expressing or finding religious impulse, motive, and meaning in the forms of comedy; and an implicit assumption that a basis for believing in the value of life can be found in the fact of comic expression itself."[1] Pritchett's attitude toward the human comedy is unequivocally tolerant and compassionate. But this generosity of spirit toward his characters never falsifies their natures or sentimentalizes their behavior, and they are made to exist in a trying, emotionally hazardous world.

In his late stories, those written in roughly the past 25 years, Pritchett's comic vision has tended, in the words of Walter Allen, "to expand in scope and to deepen in penetration."[2] The early stories are delightful for their wit and whimsy and for the way the author brings to life unusual characters, people verging on the eccentric. What the late stories have lost in quaintness and humor, however, they have gained in psychological sub-

This previously unpublished essay was written expressly for this volume.

tlety and depth and in formal organization.

Eudora Welty has observed that as Pritchett has grown older his fiction has focused increasingly on erotic love. Asked in an interview conducted when he was nearly 80 why he chose to return repeatedly in his stories to the subject of sexual love, Pritchett replied that nothing else plays such a central role in human experience or reveals more clearly the ambivalent or even contradictory levels of one's character. The mystery of character fascinates him. He said, "I never see people as being consistent with themselves at all. . . . We are what we are, but often we imagine ourselves as something else and it's that which I'm considering [in my fiction]."[3] Being an avowed psychological realist, a writer attempting to apprehend the shifting, complex configurations of common feelings, Pritchett obviously found it natural to utilize the erotic as a means of exploring the unacknowledged, ambiguous divisions of the self. What he discovers—the revelations he offers of character—are inherently comic. In these late stories, which may be called comedies of Eros, the characters learn about their self-deceptions, hidden motives and fears, and what truly matters while the sympathetic reader smilingly recognizes the characters' imperfections and identifies with their profound humanity.

✦

In "The Diver" Pritchett manages to rework a seemingly exhausted narrative situation: an older woman initiates an inexperienced, shy young man into sexuality. The freshness of this comedy rests in part on the author's skill in dramatizing the interdependence of the central character's erotic insecurities and his paralyzed literary imagination. By the story's end the tensions surrounding sexuality and art are simultaneously resolved.

The first-person narrator is looking back whimsically to the time when he was a naive 20-year-old who had come to Paris from London to become a writer. What he recalls most clearly are his frustrated literary ambitions and his sexual awkwardness and innocence. Though bursting with stories, he is inexplicably blocked from putting them down on paper. Like so many of Pritchett's characters, he is a prudish puritan and his distorted understanding of sexuality and uneasiness with women influence all his perceptions of Paris, which in his imagination is suffused with a vague lasciviousness. The evils of the flesh impinge on his daily life in the form of Mme Chamson, a voluptuous woman who lightheartedly flirts with the men at the tannery where the protagonist works. Though fascinated by her breasts and sensual mouth, he is intimidated by her eroticism and compares her to a "predatory bird."

Rather like the marine diver he has been watching descend beneath the River Seine in a salvage job, the young man is unexpectedly plunged into a foreign environment, the dim, silent apartment of Mme Chamson, where the once threatening woman is marvelously transformed: "She was not the ribald, coquettish, dangerous woman who came wagging her hips to our office, not one of my Paris fantasies of sex and danger. She was simply a woman."[4] Divested of his anxieties, the young man becomes sexually aroused, but the experienced woman turns coquettish, feigning shock at viewing his erection and saying coyly, "That is nothing to boast about."

Moments later when summoned to Mme Chamson's bedroom, the narrator is transfixed by the woman's nakedness and provocative pose. He suddenly perceives in the reality before him the essence of all the mysterious, forbidden eroticism he has fantasized about in Paris: "All the fantasies of my walks about Paris as I practiced French rushed into my head. This was the secret of all those open windows of Paris. . . . In a room like this . . . was enacted—what? Everything" (365). Questioned by the perceptive married woman whether he has ever seen a naked woman before, the young man is at first panicky and speechless. To escape the woman's anticipated emasculating laughter, the would-be writer, with desperate imagination, invents a detailed story so convincing that Mme Chamson is unnerved. With the nude Frenchwoman before him, he creates a shocking tale of the strangulation of a woman he claims to have discovered naked in her London bedroom. The invention is clearly a success, for it has the effect of rendering the imposing older woman passive, almost fearful, as though considering the possibility that the storyteller himself may have been involved in the crime. With sheer narrative imagination he has banished the woman as a frightening predatory bird and Mme Chamson becomes "a soft, ordinary, decent woman" to whom he again responds with an erect phallus: "'Ah,' she laughed, pulling at my trousers. 'The diver's come up again.'" The narrator-as-older-man smilingly concludes his recollections with the understatement "Everything was changed for me after that" (368).

"The Wheelbarrow," arguably one of Pritchett's half-dozen best stories, clearly shows the seriousness of great comedy. In the course of the story the spirits of a despondent, 40-year-old divorcée are renewed. Laura, usually referred to as Miss Freshwater's niece, comes from London to her childhood home for the lugubrious purpose of cleaning out her deceased aunt's house before putting it up for sale. The five-day cleanup becomes for her an occasion reluctantly and painfully to reconsider her emotional life, a sorting out of the rubbish among her feelings.

The reader learns that Laura, high-spirited and sexually active as a girl,

had rebelled against the prevailing materialism and propriety of her bour-
geois family. She had been more interested in experiences and emotional
relationships than in possessions and consumption. But when it came to
marrying the man she loved, Laura betrayed herself: she allowed her family to pressure her into a convenient but unhappy marriage. Now at 40 she
has serious doubts about her self-worth. Her keen resentment against her
family, all of whom are now dead, is evidenced in the satisfaction she feels
in burning the possessions of her father and aunt. Revisiting the house itself, with its ugly associations of materialism and conventionality, cannot
evoke from Laura any tender feelings; for her the house and her past are
both lifeless.

But on the second day Laura discovers a storage trunk, the contents of
which melt her heart and recall an intimately personal past, "forgotten
years of her life, her own life, not her family's." Standing over the trunk,
which contains the history of a 10-year period when she felt full of vitality
and hope, she is nearly overwhelmed by a feeling of irrecoverable loss:
"She thought she was going to be sick or faint for the past drumming, like
a train coming nearer and nearer, in her head" (123). The old photographs
she examines deeply disturb her because they thrust on her an unresting
existential truth: "But what pierced her was that in each picture of herself
she was just out of reach, flashing and yet dead; and that it was the *things*
that burned in the light of permanence. . . . They had lasted and were ageless, and she was not" (122). This disquieting awareness of human
mutability prompts Laura to consider how self-pitying and bitter she has
become and prepares for a significant change in her outlook at the end.
Seeing her face in a mirror, she is horrified at her appearance: "Not once, in
all those photographs, had a face so wolfish with bitterness and without
laughter looked back at her" (123). But she—and the reader—is about to
chuckle if not laugh at the outrageous, lustful behavior of her helper in the
cleanup.

Evans, an irrepressible evangelical preacher who is more interested in
caressing her body than in saving her soul, inadvertently contributes to
Laura's self-renewal. To Laura's surprise the born-again Christian signals
that he finds her sexually attractive and she finds herself involved in an
erotic game she has not played in years. Although ultimately she rejects his
proposition that they make love, explaining she is beyond such sexual adventures, Laura is deeply gratified to hear Evans declare that she is a radiant, golden woman with whom he cannot trust himself. She appreciates
that she is not in fact beyond such adventures, that her erotic life is not
closed. As Evans's sexual pressures on her increase, she deflects the con-

summate hypocrite's advances by figuratively throwing in his path a wheelbarrow he has coveted, a maneuver that fits deftly with the story's underlying theme of materialism.

Laura recognizes that the cleanup has been a liberating experience, a spiritual purging and recharging. Significantly, she not only burns the nostalgic black trunk but, before leaving for London, destroys the last vestiges of her sentimental, sterile past—the photograph and old love letter she had temporarily salvaged. Later as she is leaving town and hears Evans preaching against her from a revival tent, she is forgiving and can smile, knowing he helped in restoring some of her self-confidence as a woman. Most important, Laura is facing the future with a new attitude: "She knew that the happiness she felt was not ebbing, but had changed to a feeling she had not had for many years: the feeling of expectancy" (129).

The dynamics of love in "The Wedding" remind one of D. H. Lawrence without the tendentious baggage of the novelist's erotic doctrine. In this story Pritchett dramatizes the subterranean power of sexuality to overcome seemingly unbridgeable cultural differences separating two strong-willed individuals who appear temperamentally and socially unsuited for each other. Whereas many writers employ the theme of misalliance in their fiction, Pritchett is fond of successfully bringing together in love the most improbable people.

Mrs. Jackson, a divorcée in her early thirties, is a self-possessed, rather prim intellectual who teaches French in a local college. She is a self-made woman, one of many characters in Pritchett's work who, in the author's words, "invent themselves." Christine Tilly (Mrs. Jackson) realized her dream of escaping from her impoverished working-class background by passing herself off as a member of a French émigré family descended from the Comte de Tillet. She eloped with a wealthy society man and lived for a dozen years as putative duchess in high society before her marriage ended suddenly in scandal. During her marriage this bogus descendant of French aristocracy continued imaginatively to invent herself. She succeeded in time to transform herself from an ignorant girl into an educated woman knowledgeable in French literature, one able to write a biography of a kindred spirit, Mme Catherine de Rambouillet.

Tom Fletcher, who defensively calls Mrs. Jackson "the little bitch from the college," is an energetic, intelligent farmer but one who is anti-intellectual and unsophisticated to the point of being crude. He finds the woman, one of his daughter's teachers, sexually alluring; he fatuously imagines her astringent demeanor to be rooted in a lack of sexual satisfaction. Pritchett depicts Fletcher as a man in touch with the animal reality of life. The farmer treats Mrs. Jackson almost as one of his cows, swatting her affectionately on the buttocks and lassoing her around the waist, and like some gentle beast he ultimately comes to her part of the pasture "to do a deal"—that is, to take her to his farm as his mate.

Pritchett, however, is not setting up a simplistic conflict between instinct and intellect. Fletcher may be mostly animal, but Mrs. Jackson is an intellectual with real if hidden sensuality. Although she pretends to be put off by the farmer's barnyard manner, an inner, secret part of her nature finds Fletcher an exhilarating, seductive man. Her public indignation notwithstanding, she actually likes being roped and marked by Fletcher at his daughter's wedding. What this self-made woman objects to is being just another lassoed cow in a herd.

Mrs. Jackson is forced by an experience in her own house to recognize that Fletcher possesses a compelling sexual magnetism, and his inexorable erotic presence sweeps aside her genteel sophistication: "In the cottage room the short man seemed to shut out the afternoon light. He was looking into her small blue eyes and she saw he dismissed the fight in them and in her chin. . . . She put on a face of horror that gave a twist to her parted lips, but the horror was growing into a pleasure itself. It heated and was growing into a noise in her head as he stared at her" (519). Then and there the college teacher and the farmer make love on the floor of the woman's cottage. Soon afterward Mrs. Jackson gives up the intellectual milieu of the college for life on the farm, with all that that implies.

For Pritchett all love appears to be in some sense blind, unpredictable, confusing, but in "Blind Love"—a very long and complex character study—blindness itself becomes an effective central metaphor as it applies to both main characters. Leonard Armitage, a successful barrister many years divorced, has been blind for 22 years. After he falls passionately in love with his secretary, Mrs. Helen Johnson, he becomes figuratively blind too as he irrationally gives himself over to a patently fraudulent faith healer in the hope of having his sight restored. That Armitage is somewhere between an agnostic and an atheist indicates the degree of his desperation. He becomes obsessed with *seeing* the woman he loves. His jealousy is boundless for those men—including the faith healer, who avails himself of the opportunity to be a Peeping Tom—who have looked on the face and flesh of Helen Johnson.

The irony is that Mrs. Johnson, who is disfigured by an enormous birthmark on her upper body, attempts *not* to be looked on by men in an erotic way, and initially in her lovemaking with Armitage she feels relieved he is blind. There is, however, a contradictory side to this deeply sensual, 39-year-old woman. Because of an uncommon sensitivity to and anomalous indulgence of her body, she would also like her body viewed and appreciated by her sex partners, and she comes to resent it that her blind lover cannot see her. The narrator underscores her wholly believable ambivalence: "She began to be vain of the stain on her body;...she was paying him out for not being able to see her; and when she was ashamed of doing this the shame itself would rouse her desire; two women uniting in her" (238).

Blindness is also a metaphor for the woman's anxiety about expressing love. She refuses to see that her feelings for Armitage have over time become more than superficial erotic satisfactions. Sometime after Armitage has declared his love for her, she is afraid to acknowledge her true feelings: "'I admire you,' she said. She dreaded the word 'love'" (247). This dread is linked to having once been "blinded by love" for a man who later became her husband and who subsequently rejected and abandoned her when he discovered her disfigurement.

However different they are in temperament and cultural background, Mrs. Johnson and Armitage have both been deeply shamed by their physical afflictions. In their individual ways they feel flawed and defective in the core of their beings. Their bodily handicaps have partly crippled them psychologically. Much of the satisfaction in reading "Blind Love" lies in appreciating how Pritchett delicately suggests the distorting consequences of physical defects and shame on attitudes and motivations.

If Armitage and his secretary have been emotionally maimed, they have not succumbed to being mere victims of life's injustice who sigh with self-pity. Both exhibit an emotional resiliency and a sensitive pride. On one level they have come to terms with their respective circumstances—but not entirely. Both pretend to a normality that does not apply to them. For example, although Armitage cannot deny the fact of his blindness, he employs various devices to suggest to others that he actually sees what sighted people see, that he leads more or less a "normal life." For Mrs. Johnson the situation is somewhat different, in that she can better conceal her disability, yet for her too "normality has been a craving ever since childhood."

Mrs. Johnson's concealment and deceptions with men—having sex without undressing—and Armitage's elaborate systems to function as though sighted are understandable denials of reality and they periodically fail. The woman's secret will almost inevitably be exposed in a lasting relationship, and the blind man occasionally stumbles into a disorienting space that renders him helpless. The unconditional love that develops between these two hurt souls obviates the need to pretend or deceive. After Mrs. Johnson has been provoked by the unctuous faith healer to declare her love for Armitage and has purged herself of an absurd guilt for not telling him of her birthmark, Armitage terminates his absurd quest to regain his vision. In the story's coda we find that Armitage has permitted his beloved to be his eyes and interpreter of the sights of Italy and that Mrs. Johnson, experiencing the security of love, feels "gaudy" with him.

For Pritchett, born in 1900, one is never too old for erotic love, and as he aged he began writing a number of comedies of Eros among the elderly. These stories capture the feel and texture of life for those who are old. And these unsentimental, affecting stories are different from earlier comedies in at least one respect: the pressure of passing time and death's palpable presence touches them with a faint melancholy.

In "The Skeleton" Eros, in the form of a large maternal woman, barges unannounced into the life of an 82-year-old curmudgeon who has sought, out of fear and diffidence, to remain detached from authentic life and untouched by love. George Clark is a timid, scholarly man who lives defensively by anticipating unpleasantness. He judges the world a hostile, threatening place and considers each day a skirmish he sets out to win. Victory is possible only by holding the world at bay and insulating himself from others. He takes perverse pride in being a skeleton. He tells his valet, with a kind of climatic mithridatism, "The north wind doesn't touch me. There's no fat on me. I'm all bones. I'm a skeleton, there's nothing for it to bite on" (291). In fact, George's emotional self has become emaciated, and spiritually he is nearly dead.

This is not, however, the whole truth about George Clark, and Pritchett won't give up on his cantankerous character. Though George plays at being self-sufficient and cranky, he is really a victim of protracted loneliness who has grown inept at establishing emotional connections.

Suddenly into George's austere, circumscribed life comes Gloria Archer, a sensual, spontaneous woman of 50 who functions as George's nemesis and, ultimately, his savior. Always nervous in the company of women, George is especially disturbed by Gloria's unexpected visit because she brings with her, in the form of old letters of a mutual friend, the past George has tried to forget. The letters and Gloria herself recall a time when "his heart had been invaded, and he had been exposed once to a situation in which the question of victory or defeat vanished" (307). George's response to the letters he samples indicates he has become a Scrooge of love and friendship: "The letters contained, to him, the afflicting fact that he had not after all succeeded in owning his own life and closing it to others;

that he existed in other people's minds and that all people dissolved in this way, becoming fragments of one another and nothing in themselves. He had known that once, when Jack had brought him to life. He knew, too, that he had once lived or nearly lived" (305–6).

In the wonderfully comic scene of reunion George and Gloria talk at cross-purposes as she recalls the good old days and sloshes down gins while he cautions her not to make a mess. After Gloria passes out, the narrator combines a number of George's mental associations as a way of revealing how he had become a grotesque. Sitting beside the sleeping woman, the misogynist George unfairly blames Gloria for paralyzing the artistic talent of Flitestone, George's favorite painter, and driving him to suicide 25 years earlier. He associates the palpable fleshiness of the woman with his lecherous father, who "had paralyzed the whole family" and "killed their hearts" (312). The father is remembered as a sexual monster who crippled the ability of his children to love. Unexpectedly the skeleton is faced with a frightful insight: "For a moment, George left these memories and went off into anecdotes about how he fought back against his father, sniffing triumphantly, as he did at the club. But the sight of Gloria there smashed the anecdotal in him. He recognized that he had *not* fought back and had *not* been victorious. He had been whipped into the life of a timid, self-absorbed scholar" (312).

When George awakens that night from a nightmare connected to this belated self-understanding, he finds Gloria fussing over him like a solicitous wife. He becomes terrified when he imagines she might slip into his bed, the only one in the apartment:

> "Gloria," he stammered in terror of her large eyes. She came closer and sat on the bed. She took his free hand.
>
> "You're cold," she said.
>
> "No," he said. "I'm not. All bone, you see, skeleton. My sister . . ."
>
> She stood up and then bent over him and kissed him.
>
> "I'll find a blanket," she said. "I'll go back to the sofa. I'm terribly sorry George. George, I really am."
>
> "Well," said George.
>
> "George, forgive me," she said and suddenly kneeled at the bed and put her arms round him. "Let me warm you."
>
> "Oh no, no. No. Awful business," said George. (314)

But Eros wins out in the end and life becomes a less awful business. Gloria stays on to live with George Clark and warm his heart, which the story's end shows has been transformed. As George admits to his arch enemy, there are few things worse than being without human contact and love.

Unlike the skeleton, Harry, the craggy old botanist in "On the Edge of the Cliff," has spent much of his life collecting women and refuses to cease now that he has passed the biblical three score and ten years. Harry is an impressive but absurd character who, in raging against the dying of the light, enlists the aid of Eros in his losing struggle with time. For him all women are a means of holding back the terror of nonbeing that infiltrates his consciousness. Even with the likes of the aging Daisy Pike, whom he distrusts, he experiences an intensified but comforting sense of reality. Reluctantly making conversation with Daisy, Harry "found himself enjoying this hour, despite his suspicions of her. It drove away the terrors that seemed to dissolve even the trees of the ravine. With women, nature returned to its place, the trees became real trees. One lived in a long moment in which time had stopped" (471).

The story's comedy grows out of Harry's ironic situation with Rowena and the mirroring of their extraordinary relationship in Daisy's improbable affair with Stephen. One is prompted to smile at the sexual daring of a seventyish widower who falls passionately in love with a receptive 25-year-old woman. Though the narrative implies and the reader appreciates that such an affair cannot long endure, Pritchett succeeds in persuading us that the relationship, which is erotic, not platonic, actually works. But the old man knows that their anomalous love can flourish only in a slightly doctored reality, for as the narrator observes, "There are rules for old men who are in love with young girls, all the stricter when the young girls are in love with them. It has to be played as a game" (459).

Although Harry and Rowena may be aware that they are playing a game, Pritchett suggests that, like most actors in the human comedy, they cannot view themselves accurately with detachment. The reader is amused at their mildly intolerant reaction to the true nature of Daisy and Stephen's relationship. Daisy, a woman of about 50 who once loved Harry and tried to come between him and his wife, has fallen in love with a young man at least 20 years her junior. These two old friends, who have not seen each other for years, come together by chance at a town fair in Wales. Uneasily they stand chatting as they wait, rather like impatient parents, for the return of their respective lovers, who are, suggestively, riding a merry-go-round. Harry mistakes Stephen for Daisy's son and on learning the truth is astonished and repelled by the relationship. Suggesting that they are alike in their slightly absurd situations, Daisy says to her old friend at a later meeting, "Love is something at our age, isn't it?" (471).

Harry is not amused and refuses to acknowledge they are counterparts. When he informs Rowena, who is young enough to be his granddaughter, that Stephen is Daisy's lover, her unimaginative response is this: "'You can't mean that,' she said, putting on a very proper air. 'She is old enough—' but she stopped" (473). With respect to their own preposterous but touching game, Harry and Rowena wisely concentrate on playing rather than on reflection. With typical tolerance Pritchett shows that they see their own arbitrary rules as inapplicable to other players, and yet such self-deception allows them to value their transitory passion.

Two late stories, "The Spree" and "A Trip to the Seaside," concern the way elderly men deal with loneliness owing to the loss of a mate. Though similar in theme and setting, these comedies are decidedly different in effect because of the singular characters created and the disparate tones adopted. Without a trace of sentimentality Pritchett in "The Spree" records an old man's efforts to maintain his dignity and emotional equanimity two years after suffering the shock of his wife's death. On the surface the 70-year-old retired salesman appears to be coping successfully with his loss, but he believes his days are "stacked up meaninglessly waiting for him." The opening of the story conveys the unspeakable loneliness of someone forever separated from that beloved who was once almost a part of oneself: "The old man—but when does old age begin?—the old man turned over in bed and putting out his hand to the crest of his wife's beautiful white rising hip and comforting bottom, hit the wall with his knuckles and woke up. More than once during the two years since she had died he had done this and knew that if old age vanished in the morning it came on at night, filling the bedroom with people until, switching on the light, he saw it staring at him; then it shuffled off and left him looking at the face of the clock" (395). He realizes that for two years his life has been in abeyance, that his grief has prevented him from divesting himself of "an increasing load of unsaid things, . . . things he had no one to tell" (408). In his adventure that constitutes the story he meets a widow to whom he can unburden himself and he senses in this woman what he desperately needs: a loving companion.

Despite its themes of grief and loneliness, "The Spree" is not a melancholy story. On the contrary, Pritchett's tone is bright and jocular and the unnamed protagonist displays a jauntiness and buoyancy of spirit; he is simply not allowed to pause for self-pity. For example, when the old man becomes dispirited and attempts to phone his friend Frenchy, he mistakenly dials the house where he and his wife had lived. When he discovers his mistake the old man is shocked and fears he is losing his mind. This is a moment of genuine pathos, but Pritchett has no intention of holding the reader at this emotional level. Swiftly he shuffles the widower into the frenetic, holiday atmosphere of a pub, where he is indulged by a group of young people. Pritchett permits the reader to feel the grief underlying the old man's existence but shifts the focus away from it. What he does want us to appreciate is the way ordinary people, with some sense of humor or irony, manage to cope with emotional pain. And he achieves this almost entirely by controlling the narrative tone.

The old man and the woman he meets aboard the company bus have an obvious affinity for one another, and the widow, though feigning to be offended, is impressed with the man's audacity when she learns that he is not connected with the company sponsoring the bus and the party. Pritchett handles the inchoate romance of these elderly characters with great restraint. The old man, at Frenchy's urging, has considered buying his own place by the sea, and the widow owns one. After the bus reaches Brighton, she offers to drive him to her bungalow, ostensibly to show the house to him as a prospective buyer.

Her real interest, however, is in the widower himself. Significantly, she changes into a white dress patterned with red poppies before serving tea. Earlier the old man, while talking to her on the bus, thinks, "Grief—what was it? A craving. Yet not for a face or even a voice or even for love, but for a body. But dressed. Say, in a flowered dress" (408). When they part at the train station, the widow, suggestively touching the old man's drooping rose, shyly invites him to call on her whenever he is in Brighton. And in the story's final paragraphs we learn that the widow has been phoning him in the weeks following their meeting and that the old man is planning to visit her, knowing "that what he needed was not a house" or independence from his son's family but the physical presence of a loving woman.

The self-satisfied widower in "A Trip to the Seaside" is the kind of character many writers less forgiving than Pritchett would quickly lose patience with and end up mocking or ridiculing. Mr. Andrews is certainly not villainous or repugnant, but he does display deplorable characteristics: egotism, presumptuousness, and smugness. Maintaining an ironic tone in this story, Pritchett presents his character's complacent behavior as laughable without losing sight of the man's dignity as he tries to go on with life after his wife's death. The story is not *about* grief, but the pain of this emotion lies just below the surface of the comedy. For example: "He suddenly found himself crumpling into an account of Daisy's [his wife's] long illness and death"[5] and "Since his wife's death he had taken to rambling on to local people in the shops, even in the street where he lived, to anyone, about the bemusing novelty of his new life. He could not stop himself. Grief had made him novel, and he called himself 'you'" (77).

Mr. Andrews realizes he needs another wife to care for him, but selecting a woman and winning her heart are a daunting prospect. With a wholly misplaced confidence he decides to approach Louisa Browder, his former secretary, whom he has unfortunately not seen in five years, owing to an embarrassing falling-out over sexual matters. Blocking out memory of this incident, he cannot imagine that the woman he remembers as nervous, cringing, and dutiful would not be erotically available to him.

The story's central irony—that Mr. Andrews presumes Louisa is still a spinster when, in fact, she is happily married—is enriched by the reader's understanding that the former carpet salesman considers the woman below his standards, "a *faute de mieux*." He is plainly a snob. Regardless of his misgivings, Louisa is the *only* eligible woman he knows. Furthermore, because he feels superior to her, she is a safe, unthreatening choice, unlike all the formidable women out there in the world who might rebuff him, who "might slap your face if you stopped them and explained your situation" (79).

Mr. Andrews's assumed advantage over Louisa crumbles almost as soon as he sees her. He finds that she has significantly changed in five years, has become relaxed, confident, and attractive. When she tells him she is not, as he assumed, living in a dowdy bed-and-breakfast but, rather, in a first-class hotel, her perceived value increases. He thinks, "Hotels were palaces of pleasure and money. Their very upholstery sent messages of erotic sensation when one touched it" (80). As their conversation continues, he senses that the woman he had come to visit unannounced and had taken for granted in a broader sense may not in fact be at his disposal.

When he learns what the reader has already surmised, that Louisa is married, Mr. Andrews loses his composure and experiences a kind of emotional impotence. Feeling betrayed by a former "office possession," he immediately understands what Louisa's unavailability means to him. Now he has no prospect for another woman and his loneliness will be prolonged indefinitely: "It seemed to him that she was not one woman but had become part of the general chorus of women he had seen in the streets of the town, impersonally swinging their handbags and lugging their shopping bags, taunting him with their indifference" (83). So disorienting has the revelation of Louisa's marriage been that he considers how his dead wife will react when she is told.

At this point Pritchett deepens the irony of Mr. Andrews's situation. Five years earlier he had an erotic opportunity with Louisa. Just as the suspicious, jealous Daisy had warned, the secretary one festive night tried to seduce him in a hotel. Startled and confused, he had deflected her advance by appearing obtuse and invoking his wife's name. Mr. Andrews recalls this event as a moment of "inadmissible desire," whereas Louisa remembers it with anger and chagrin. The night after this awkward incident the salesman was flabbergasted to discover another man in her hotel room, "the rival" who later would marry her and, as it turned out, leave him defeated and forlorn.

"A Trip to the Seaside" ends where it began—only the first three paragraphs and last sentence and a half are written in the fictional present—aboard a London-bound train carrying Mr. Andrews away from the seaside and his stillborn hopes. Dejected and more lonely than ever, he hears the wheels of the train rhythmically repeating "nothing" as he sits "alone, looking blankly at the villas, trees, and fields wheeling back in the watery spring dusk" (70).

✦

In the eight representative comedies discussed here and in other late stories, Pritchett shows why he is regarded as one of the finest, most engaging short-story writers of our time. Like scores of accomplished writers, he is technically proficient and a keen observer of life and human nature, but what raises Pritchett to a higher level is his ability, in story after story, to persuade the reader willingly to cooperate with him, to respond in the depths of his or her imagination to where the author is leading. Some of this may be ascribed to pure literary technique. But there is more here. The reader intuitively feels that the stories are rooted in a compassionate intelligence about life, a real wisdom that comes from experience. Behind Pritchett's fiction lies a palpably humane presence, a moral mind.

Notes

1. Robert M. Polhemus, *Comic Faith: The Great Tradition from Austen to Joyce* (Chicago: University of Chicago Press, 1980), 3.

2. Walter Allen, *The Short Story in English* (Oxford: Clarendon Press, 1981), 274.

3. Douglas A. Hughes, "V. S. Pritchett: An Interview," *Studies in Short Fiction* 13 (Fall 1976): 429.

4. *Collected Stories* (New York: Random House, 1982), 363. Unless otherwise indicated, subsequent references to Pritchett's stories are from this volume.

5. "Trip to the Seaside," *A Careless Widow and Other Stories* (New York: Random House, 1989), 76. All remaining citations are from this volume.

Eudora Welty

This great and fascinating writer is about the age of our century and has written short stories most of his way through it. With their abundance, they are of equally remarkable variety: Where would one look for the typical Pritchett story? But one always finds this—that any Pritchett story is all of it alight and busy at once, like a well-going fire. Wasteless and at the same time well fed, it shoots up in flame from its own spark like a poem or a magic trick, self-consuming, with nothing left over. He is one of the great pleasure givers in our language.

Pritchett himself has said that the short story is his greatest love because he finds it challenging. The new collection makes it clear that neither the love nor the challenge has let him down.

As ever, the writing spouts with energy. Dialogue, in constant exchange, frisks like a school of dolphin. These are *social* stories: Life goes on in them without flagging. The characters that fill them—erratic, unsure, unsafe, devious, stubborn, restless and desirous, absurd and passionate, all peculiar unto themselves—hold a claim on us that is not to be denied. They demand and get our rapt attention, for in their revelation of their lives, the secrets of our own lives come into view. How much the eccentric has to tell us of what is central!

Once more, in the present volume, the characters are everything. Through a character Pritchett can trace a trail thread of chivalry in the throatcutting trade of antique collecting. Through a character he finds a great deal of intrigue in old age. The whole burden of "The Spree" is grief and what his character is ever to do with it. Paradox comes naturally to Pritchett, and he has always preferred, and excelled in, the oblique approach; and I think all these varying stories in today's book are love stories.

One is called "The Diver." Panicking as his initiation into sex confronts him in the middle-aged Frenchwoman lying "naked and idle" on her bed—who mocks him with "You have never seen a woman before?"—the young English boy is surprised by his own brain beginning to act: He hears himself begin answering her with, a preposterous lie. He is into another initiation—he is becoming a story writer as he stands there quaking. "It

"A Family of Emotions" (review of *Selected Stories*) by Eudora Welty, *New York Times Book Review*, 25 June 1978, 1, 39–40. © 1978 by The New York Times Co. Reprinted by permission.

was her turn to be frightened." All being squared, the woman back in her earlier character of "a soft, ordinary, decent woman," that is when his heart begins to throb. "And everything was changed for me after this."

Of these 14 stories—chosen from four volumes published over the last nine years—"The Diver" is not the only one here to suggest that, in times of necessity or crisis, a conspiracy may form among the deep desires of our lives to substitute for one another, to masquerade sometimes as one another, to support, to save one another. These stories seem to find that human desire is really a *family* of emotions, a whole interconnection—not just the patriarch and matriarch, but all the children. All kin, and none of them born to give up. If anything happens to cut one off, they go on surviving in one another's skins. They become something new. In fact, they become storytellers.

In "Blind Love," when Mr. Armitage employs Mrs. Johnson, two people have been brought together who have been afflicted beyond ordinary rescue. Mr. Armitage is blind; Mrs. Johnson has a very extensive and horrifying birthmark. Beneath her clothes, "She was stamped with an ineradicable bloody insult." When she was young and newly married, her husband had sent her packing for the horror of its surprise, for her having thus "deceived" him. Now, "as a punished and self-hating person, she was drawn to work with a punished man. It was a return to her girlhood: Injury had led her to injury." In the love affair that grows out of this doubleness, blindness and deceiving are played against each other, are linked together—as though each implied the other. How much does each really know? We watch to see what hurt does to vision—or *for* vision; what doubt does to faith, faith to doubt. These two magnetized people have selves hidden under selves; they have more than one visible or invisible skin. After they reach and survive a really fatal crisis of ambiguous revelation, the only possible kind, we see them contentedly traveling in tandem. "She has always had a secret. It still pleases Armitage to baffle people." But they are matched now in "blind love." They depend on each other altogether.

"The Marvellous Girl" is a double portrait. One side is blind love, love in the dark. The obverse side is a failed marriage in clear view. (It failed because "even unhappiness loses its tenderness and fascination.") A husband, from the back of a large audience, can see his wife seated on a stage in the glare of the light and the public eye, "a spectator of his marriage that had come to an end." She looks "smaller and more bizarre." When the lights suddenly go out in the auditorium, the darkness "extinguished everything. It stripped the eyes of sight. . . . One was suddenly naked in the dark from the boots upward. One could feel the hair on one's body growing and in the chatter one could hear men's voices grunting, women's voices fast, breath going in and out, muscles changing, hearts beating. Many people stood up. Surrounded by animals like himself he too stood up, to hunt with the pack, to get out."

On the stairs he comes by accident up against his wife: "He heard one of the large buttons on his wife's coat click against a button on his coat. She was there for a few seconds: It seemed to him as long as their marriage."

Still in the dark, and like a dream, comes his discovery—it is his pursuit—of "the marvellous girl." And afterward, when the lights come on again, "they got up, scared, hot-faced, hating the light. 'Come on. We must get out,' he said. And they hurried from the lighted room to get into the darkness of the city."

We read these stories, comic or tragic, with an elation that stems from their intensity. In "When My Girl Comes Home" Pritchett establishes a mood of intensification that spreads far around and above it like a brooding cloud, far-reaching, not promising us to go away. We are with a family in England 10 years after the last World War as they face the return of a daughter, gone all this time, who is thought to be a prisoner of the enemy. Hilda, "rescued" at last from Japan, where she had not, after all, been tortured and raped but had done very well for herself, brings on a shock as excruciating as it is gradual when her shifting and cheapening tales begin to come out.

The youngest boy muses. "We must have all known in our different ways that we had been disturbed in a very long dream. We had been living on inner visions for years. It was an effect of the long war. England had been a prison. Even the sky was closed, and, like convicts, we had been driven to dwelling on fancies in our dreary minds. "In the cinema," he says, and that cloud begins to reach overhead, "the camera sucks some person forward into an enormous close-up and holds a face three yards wide, filling the whole screen, all holes and pores, like some sucking octopus that might eat up an audience rows at a time. . . . Hilda had been a close-up like this for us when she was lost and far away."

In the shock of reunion, the whole family—several generations and their connections—sees appearing, bit by bit, the evidence that all of them have been marred, too, have been driven, are still being driven and still being changed by the same war. Alone and collectively, they have become calloused as Hilda has been and, in some respect of their own, made monsters by their passage through an experience too big for them, as it was too big for Hilda—for anyone.

"Hilda had been our dream, but now she was home she changed as fast as dreams change," the boy tells us. "She was now, as we looked at her, far more remote to us than she had been all the years when she was away."

Finally, it is not Hilda's errant life in Japan but the "rescue," the return to the family circle, that wrecks her imperviousness. It wrecks the life at home, too. When the young narrator finds himself alone at the end with Hilda, "I wanted to say more. I wanted to touch her. But I couldn't. The ruin had made her untouchable."

None of the stories is livelier than these new stories of Pritchett's written of old age. Old bachelor clubman George is militant, astringent, biting, fearsomely grinning, in training with his cold baths, embattled behind his fossilized anecdotes, victoriously keeping alive ("he got up every day to win") on the adrenalin of outrage and of constituting himself a trial and a bore to everyone. But afraid. Afraid not of the North wind but of the East wind, afraid not that the Arch Enemy will get him but that the building will be sold out from under him:

> "O God," he groaned loudly, but in a manner so sepulchral and private that people moved respectfully away. It was a groan that seemed to come up from the earth, up from his feet, a groan of loneliness that was raging and frightening to the men around him. He had one of those moments when he felt dizzy, when he felt he was lost among unrecognizable faces, without names, alone, in the wrong club, at the wrong address even, with the tottering story of his life, a story which he was offering or, rather, throwing out as a lifeline for help.

What wins out over George is not the East wind or the Arch Enemy but the warm arms of a large, drinking, 40-year-old woman with a kind of disposition and a giggle for his indignation, who "drops in" ("What manners!") out of his past that he had thought safely sealed behind anecdotes. She was the woman the old man had admired once "for being so complete an example of everything that made women impossible."

It is thus that he faces "the affronting fact that he had not after all succeeded in owning his own life and closing it to others; that he existed in other people's minds and that all people dissolved in this way, becoming fragments of one another, and nothing in themselves. . . . He knew, too, that he had once lived, or nearly lived."

Of all the stories of desiring, and of all the stories in this collection, "The Camberwell Beauty" is the most marvelous. It is a story of desiring and also of possessing—we are in a world of antique-shop keepers—and of possessing that survived beyond the death of desiring. It is a closed world, one that has its own hours, its own landscape inside nighttime warehouses, its edges the streets beneath the sodium lights. It has its own breed of people, its own language, its codes and spies and secrets and shames, jealousies, savageries, fantasies. And like some fairy tale itself, it has its own maiden, carried off and shut up and, you and I would think, wanting to accept rescue, but provided with a bugle to play if this should threaten.

"It broke my heart to think of that pretty girl living among such people and drifting into the shabbiness of the trade," says the young man—he is also of the trade—who discovers her and loses her when an old man named Pliny carries her off for himself and shuts her up in his shop. The boy cannot forget how she had written her name in the dust of a table top and left it unfinished: "I S A B—half a name, written by a living finger in the dust."

The young man is left "with a horror of the trade I had joined." He abhors "the stored up lust that seemed to pass between things and men like Pliny." It is not long before "the fever of the trade had come alive in me: Pliny had got something I wanted." The end is unescapable—for all, that is, who are connected with the trade.

"The Camberwell Beauty" is an extraordinary piece of work. Densely complex and unnervingly beautiful in its evocation of those secret, packed rooms, it seems to shimmer with the gleam of its unreliable treasures. There is the strange device of the bugle—which, blown by Isabel, actually kills desire. All the while the story is filled with longing, it remains savage and seething and crass and gives off the unhidable smell of handled money.

Most extraordinarily of all, it expresses, not the confusion of one human desire with another, not sexuality confused with greed, but rather the culmination of these desires in their *fusion.*

"How unreal people looked in the sodium light," the defeated boy thinks as he walks in the street at the story's end. Or by the light of their obsessions.

Each story's truth is distilled by Pritchett through a pure concentration of human character. It is the essence of his art. And, of course, in plain fact, and just as in a story, it is inherent in the human being to create his own situation, his own plot. The paradoxes, the stratagems, the escapes, the entanglements, the humors and dreams, are all projections of the individual human being, all by himself alone. In its essence, Pritchett's work, so close to fantasy, is deeply true to life.

William Trevor

Everyone likes V. S. Pritchett, people say, and everyone respects his achievement. He has been honored by his fellow writers on both sides of the Atlantic. He has been rewarded by the British establishment: Sir Victor Pritchett is nowadays his title. You could call him the Grand Old Man of English letters and he himself might not even object.

Yet all of that has a faint blandness about it, which does not reflect a unique and highly personal literary talent. Nor is it a help to be reminded that V. S. Pritchett the short-story writer is also a novelist, travel writer, lecturer, and critic: such lists, somehow, don't suit this quiet writer. The truth is that in order to discover the essential Pritchett you have to read your way through him; and above all you have to read his short stories.

"To put together," he writes in his preface to this present volume,

a substantial if not complete collection of the stories from the seven volumes I have written in the last fifty years is a startling experience in old age. One comes across a procession of vanished selves. In what room, in what town or country, did I write them? In what chair was I sitting and where did I get this or that fragment of a scene or a character? I see a crowd of old friends, too. How did the story change as I re-wrote it, perhaps four or five times, boiling down a hundred pages into twenty or thirty, as I still do? Story writing is exacting work. I fancy if I took each story sentence by sentence, I would find the now mingled minutes of personal experience taken arbitrarily from events or feelings (which in reality were far apart in my own life) had been turned by art into something else. How was it that a commercial traveller in Enniskillen turned into another in the English Midlands and who told his own vernacular story when I had written it all before as an impersonal study?

No one alive today comments as valuably about the short story as Pritchett does, and that is because he perfectly understands the form through his own dealings in it. Repeatedly his writing reminds you how satisfying a good short story is, how much *more* satisfying than an only slightly flawed novel. His art, and his craft, hover high above the big, loose novels of our time, which so often are empty of everything except their

"Pritchett Proclaimed" (review of Collected Stories) by William Trevor, New Republic, 2 August 1982, 30–32. © 1982 by The New Republic, Inc. Reprinted by permission of the New Republic.

own complications. "I was really attracted to concision," he writes, "... reducing possible novels to essentials. I love the intricacy of the short form, the speed with which it can change from scene to scene. I have always thought that the writer of short stories is a mixture of reporter, aphoristic wit, moralist and poet—though not 'poetical'; he is something of a ballad-maker, and in the intricacy of his design is close to the writer of sonnets."

Pritchett's brilliance, I believe, emerges from this understanding of his own gift. He knows instinctively, as neither D. H. Lawrence nor Joyce knew, that the shorter form was the one to master, that that is where his voice is. It is fashionable to suggest that the contents of *Dubliners* is slight stuff compared with the teeming architecture of *Ulysses* or *Finnegans Wake*. I believe the opposite to be true, and I believe that Lawrence wrote no novel as impressive as "The Rocking-Horse Winner" or "The Man Who Loved Islands."

✦

Pritchett captures the explosion of truth, as in an Impressionist painting, and the excitement of that task has deliberately been allowed to obsess him, while excursions at greater length have come to take the form of autobiographical reminiscence or critical comment. Devotion to his chosen form is evident everywhere in his stories, from the very earliest to the contents of *On the Edge of the Cliff*, his last collection. Invisible technique conveys a mood, arranges the flow of narrative, selects, prunes, discards, retains, insistently gets everything right. And it's this "getting things right" that is so vital in short stories: there can be no approximation, no doubt, no meandering or self-indulgence. Plot is not a vital ingredient, but there must always be a point. A story without one—and far too many contemporary stories do have such a lack—is like an apple tree that never fruits. In the best sense of the term, Pritchett is fruity.

In "Many are Disappointed," four men, cycling through the English countryside, arrive at what they imagine to be a public house. Bert, the youngest, has been dreaming as he pedaled: "You get to the pub, and there's a girl at the pub, a dark girl with bare arms and bare legs in a white frock, the daughter of the house or an orphan—maybe it's better she should be an orphan—and you say something to her, or, better still, you don't say anything to her—she comes and puts her arms around you, and you can feel her skin through her frock and she brings you some beer and the other chaps aren't there."

But the house they've arrived at isn't the tavern it claims to be, the thirsty travelers have to make do with tea, the woman who's there has a vacant look, with hair of an "impure yellow" and a smile from a faded photograph. The men are disappointed but the reader has been seized by the mystery of the place and is not going to leave it until Pritchett permits him to. Yet all of it, at first glance, is ordinary enough: "They looked at the room. There were two new treacle-coloured armchairs. There was a sofa with a pattern of black ferns on it. The new plush was damp and sticky to the hands from the air of the hidden sea. There was a gun-metal fender and there was crinkled green paper in the fireplace. A cupboard with a glass door was empty except for the lowest shelf. On that was a thick book called *The Marvels of Science.*"

England, unlike Russia, America, or Ireland, is not noted for its fascination with the short story. There have been Kipling, of course, and Coppard and de la Mare. Somerset Maugham wrote poor novels and superb stories; Lawrence I've mentioned. But English fiction ever since Jane Austen has been dominated by the novel, a form particularly suitable as a mirror in the rich, settled Victorian society that spawned it: easily established then, it has thrived since. Yet a foreigner, wishing to understand the England of the last fifty years, and to understand the English themselves, might profitably turn first to the stories of V. S. Pritchett. He would meet such excessively local figures as Mrs. Forster of the scented Edwardian voice, and the colonel's daughter and Mr. Timberlake of the Church of the Last Purification, and Gentleman Pliny, and Mrs. Prosser who looks like a fist. He would meet the prejudices and prettinesses of that extraordinary island, the subtleties of its class system, the trailing mists of an empire that will not quite go away.

Pritchett's Englishness is notable. It has developed through his interest in countries not his own; Spain and Ireland have been favorite places, but in a long life he has been alertly agog wherever he has gone, journeying in the United States or behind the Iron Curtain or simply crossing the English Channel. He has an ear for anecdotes which explain not only the natives he visits, but the natives he has left behind: one's own country can often be seen more clearly from a distance, and travelers traveling nervously are grist for the fiction writer's mill. Pritchett's "Handsome Is as Handsome Does," concerned with an English couple abroad, is in this respect an astonishing tour de force. It catches two unattractive people at their most vulnerable, working up in the reader a gradual sympathy for their mundane plight. One ends by discovering in them qualities which it seemed at first quite impossible that they should possess. They remain physically ugly, shabby, and somewhat embarrassing, but they have been touched with human dignity: one should, of course, have known that it was there all the time.

The more parochial and domestic these stories appear to be on the surface the deeper the depths they acquire when considered in retrospect. Pritchett writes of the universal by way of a narrow particular, allowing humor and the variations in human relationships to create his patterns of truth. He has done more for the short story in his lifetime than anyone since Joyce or Chekhov. He has probably done more for the English short story than anyone has ever done.

Chronology

1900	Victor Sawdon Pritchett born in Ipswich, Suffolk, 16 December, first child of Walter and Beatrice (Martin) Pritchett.
1916	Is removed from school by his father and sent to London to work in the leather trade.
1920–1923	Works in the shellac, glue, and photographic trades in Paris; sells sketches to British weeklies and to the *Christian Science Monitor*.
1923–1926	Is correspondent in Ireland and Spain for the *Christian Science Monitor*.
1926	Publishes first story, "Rain in the Sierra," in the *New Statesman*.
1927	Edward J. O'Brien selects "Tragedy in a Greek Theatre" for republication in *Best Short Stories of the Year (1927)*.
1928	Publishes first book, *Marching Spain* (travel).
1929	Publishes first novel, *Clare Drummer*.
1930	Publishes first collection of stories, *The Spanish Virgin*, which sells better than expected.
1932	*Shirley Sanz* (novel).
1935	*Nothing like Leather* (novel).
1936	Marries Dorothy Roberts; "Sense of Humour" published by John Lehmann in *New Writing*.
1937	*Dead Man Leading* (novel); becomes permanent critic for the *New Statesman*.
1938	*You Make Your Own Life* (story collection); daughter Josephine born.
1939	"Pocock Passes" is selected for *Best British Short Stories (1939)*.

1940	Son Oliver born; "The Saint" is selected for *Best British Short Stories (1940)*.
1942	*In My Good Books* (critical essays).
1945	*It May Never Happen* (story collection); becomes literary editor of the *New Statesman*.
1948	Edits *Turnstile One: A Literary Miscellany from the New Statesman; Why Do I Write?* (criticism; with Elizabeth Bowen and Graham Greene).
1949	The *New Yorker* publishes "The Ladder" and "The Landlord," the first of many Pritchett stories to appear there.
1951	*Mr. Beluncle* (novel); becomes director of the *New Statesman*.
1953	Is Christian Gauss lecturer at Princeton University; *Books in General* (criticism).
1956	*Collected Stories* (Britain); *The Sailor, Sense of Humour, and Other Stories* (United States).
1961	*When My Girl Comes Home* (story collection).
1962	*London Perceived* (travel).
1963	*The Key to My Heart* (story collection).
1966	*The Saint* (story collection).
1968	*A Cab at the Door* (autobiography).
1969	*Blind Love* (story collection); is elected Fellow, Royal Society of Literature.
1970	*George Meredith and English Comedy* (criticism).
1971	*Midnight Oil* (autobiography); is made honorary member of American Academy of Arts and Letters.
1973	*Balzac* (criticism).
1974	*The Camberwell Beauty* (story collection); is elected international president of PEN.
1975	Is knighted for services to literature.
1977	*The Gentle Barbarian: The Life and Work of Turgenev* (criticism).

1978	*Selected Stories;* receives Columbia University honorary D.Litt.
1979	*The Myth Makers: Literary Essays.*
1980	*The Tale Bearers* (criticism).
1982	*Collected Stories.*
1983	*More Collected Stories.*
1984	*The Other Side of a Frontier: A V. S. Pritchett Reader.*
1985	*A Man of Letters* (criticism).
1988	*Chekhov: A Spirit Set Free* (criticism).
1989	*A Careless Widow* (story collection); *At Home and Abroad* (travel).
1990	*Lasting Impressions* (criticism).
1991	*Complete Collected Stories* (published in Britain in 1990 as *The Complete Short Stories*).

Bibliography

Primary Works

Collections

Blind Love and Other Stories. London: Chatto & Windus, 1969; New York: Random House, 1969. Includes "Blind Love," "The Nest Builder," "A Debt of Honour," "The Cage Birds," "The Skeleton," "The Speech," "The Liars," "Our Oldest Friends," "The Honeymoon," "The Chain Smoker."

The Camberwell Beauty and Other Stories. London: Chatto & Windus, 1974; New York: Random House, 1974. Includes "The Camberwell Beauty," "The Diver" (originally published in the *New Yorker* as "The Fall"), "Did You Invite Me?," "The Rescue," "The Marvellous Girl," "The Spree," "Our Wife" (originally published as "The Captain's Daughter" in the *New Yorker*), "The Last Throw," "The Lady from Guatemala."

A Careless Widow and Other Stories. London: Chatto & Windus, 1989; New York: Random House, 1989. Includes "A Careless Widow" (originally published in the *New Yorker* as "Neighbors"), "Cocky Olly," "A Trip to the Seaside," "Things," "A Change of Policy," "The Image Trade."

Collected Stories. London: Chatto & Windus, 1956. Includes all of the stories in *You Make Your Own Life* and *It May Never Happen*, to which are added "The Sniff," "The Collection," "The Satisfactory," "The Ladder," "Passing the Ball," "Things as They Are," "The Landlord," "A Story of Don Juan," "Double Divan."

Collected Stories. London: Chatto & Windus, 1982; New York: Random House, 1982. Includes "The Sailor," "The Saint," "Many Are Disappointed," "Things as They Are," "Handsome Is as Handsome Does," "You Make Your Own Life," "The Voice," "Sense of Humour," "The Wheelbarrow," "The Fall," "When My Girl Comes Home," "Citizen," "The Key to My Heart," "Blind Love," "A Debt of Honour," "The Cage Birds," "The Skeleton," "The Speech," "The Camberwell Beauty," "The Diver," "Did You Invite Me?," "The Marvellous Girl," "The Spree," "The Lady from Guatelmala," "The Fig Tree," "On the Edge of the Cliff," "A Family Man," "Tea with Mrs. Bittell," "The Wedding."

Complete Collected Stories. New York: Random House, 1991. Consists of 82 stories—that is, all stories of all of the other volumes listed with the exception of *The Spanish Virgin*, of which none is included.

The Complete Short Stories. London: Chatto & Windus, 1990. Same as *Complete Collected Stories.*

It May Never Happen and Other Stories. London: Chatto & Windus, 1945; New York: Reynal, 1947. Includes "The Sailor," "The Lion's Den," "The Saint," "It May Never Happen," "Pocock Passes," "Oedipus Complex," "The Voice," "Aunt Gertrude," "Many Are Disappointed," "The Chestnut-Tree," "The Ape," "The Clerk's Tale," "The Fly in the Ointment," "The Night Worker."

The Key to My Heart. London: Chatto & Windus, 1963; New York: Random House, 1964. Includes "The Key to My Heart," "Noisy Flushes the Birds," "Noisy in the Doghouse."

More Collected Stories. London: Chatto & Windus, 1983; New York: Random House, 1983; New York: Vintage, 1985. Includes "Our Oldest Friend," "The Nest Builder," "The Liars," "The Rescue," "Our Wife," "The Last Throw," "The Worshippers," "The Vice-Consul," "The Evils of Spain," "The Two Brothers," "Pocock Passes," "The Oedipus Complex," "The Fly in the Ointment," "The Night Worker," "The Necklace," "The Accompanist," "On the Scent," "Double Divan," "A Story of Don Juan," "Passing the Ball," "The Landlord," "The Ladder," "The Spanish Bed," "The Satisfactory."

On the Edge of the Cliff and Other Stories. London: Chatto & Windus, 1979; New York: Random House, 1979. Includes "On the Edge of the Cliff," "A Family Man," "The Spanish Bed," "The Wedding," "The Worshippers," "The Vice-Consul," "Tea with Mrs. Bittell," "The Accompanist," "The Fig Tree."

The Sailor, Sense of Humour, and Other Stories. New York: Alfred A. Knopf, 1956. Includes "The Sailor," "The Oedipus Complex," "The Saint," "Many Are Disappointed," "Passing the Ball," "Things as They Are," "It May Never Happen," "The Landlord," "Main Road," "Handsome Is as Handsome Does," "Pocock Passes," "The Sniff," "The Scapegoat," "The Lion's Den," "Eleven O'clock," "You Make Your Own Life," "Miss Baker," "The Ape," "The Chestnut Tree," "The Evils of Spain," "The Voice," "The Fly in the Ointment," "The Night Worker," "The Satisfactory," "Sense of Humour."

The Saint and Other Stories. Harmondsworth, U.K.: Penguin, 1966. A republication of 21 of the stories of the Chatto & Windus *Collected Stories* of 1956.

Selected Stories. New York: Random House, 1978. Includes "The Diver," "The Wheelbarrow," "Blind Love," "The Fall," "The Skeleton," "When My Girl Comes Home," "Key to My Heart," "Noisy Flushes the Birds," "Noisy in the Doghouse," "The Marvellous Girl," "Cage Birds," "Camberwell Beauty," "The Spree," "The Chain-Smoker."

The Spanish Virgin and Other Stories. London: Ernest Benn, 1930. Includes "The Spanish Virgin," "Tragedy in a Greek Theatre," "The White Rabbit," "Fishy," "The Corsican Inn," "The Petrol Dump," "The Haunted Room," "Rain in the Sierra," "The Sack of Lights," "The Cuckoo Clock," "The Gnats."

Bibliography

When My Girl Comes Home. London: Chatto & Windus, 1961; New York: Alfred A. Knopf, 1961. Includes "The Wheelbarrow," "The Fall," "When My Girl Comes Home," "The Necklace," "Just a Little More," "The Snag," "On the Scent," "Citizen," "The Key to My Heart."

You Make Your Own Life. London: Chatto & Windus, 1938. Includes "Sense of Humour," "A Spring Morning," "Main Road," "The Evils Of Spain," "Handsome Is as Handsome Does," "The Aristocrat," "The Two Brothers," "X-ray," "The Scapegoat," "Eleven O'clock," "The Upright Man," "Page and Monarch," "Miss Baker," "You Make Your Own Life."

Uncollected Stories

"Agranti, for Lisbon." *Fortnightly Review*, August 1930, 235–46.

"The Ape Who Lost His Tail." *New Writing*, n.s. 1 (Autumn 1938): 233–40.

"The Chimney." *New Statesman and Nation*, 26 December 1936, 1061–63.

"Cup Final." *New Statesman and Nation*, 18 December 1943, 398–99.

"Doctor's Story." *New Statesman and Nation*, 3 January 1948, 8–9.

"The Educated Girl." *Transatlantic Review:* 5 (December 1960): 51–56. Reprinted in *Stories from the Transatlantic Review*, edited by Joseph F. McCrindle. New York: Holt, 1970.

"Father and the Bucket Shop." *Night and Day*, 23 September 1937, 12–15.

"Goldfish." *New Statesman and Nation*, 26 December 1942, 422–23.

"Hiawatha Complex." *New Statesman and Nation*, 29 December 1956, 835–36.

"In Autumn Quietly." *John o' London's Weekly*, 4 February 1933, 713–15.

"I Passed by Your Window." *London Mercury*, December 1938, 131–44.

"The Invader." *New Statesman and Nation*, 11 January 1941, 34–35.

"Jury." *Fortnightly Review*, March 1937, 321–27.

"New World." *John o' London's Weekly*, 22 December 1939, 373–74.

"A Public Benefactress." *Bystander*, 17 August 1938, 265+.

"Serious Question." *Fortnightly Review*, February 1931, 209–17.

"Slooter's Vengeance." *New Statesman and Nation*, 28 March 1931, vi–vii.

"The Truth about Mrs. Brown." *Nash's Pall Mall*, March 1936, 111–27.

"Uncle for Christmas." *News Chronicle*, 12 April 1939.

"Upstairs, Downstairs." *Night and Day*, 1 July 1937, 13–15.

"Woolly Gloves." *Fortnightly Review*, June 1931, 804–16. Reprinted in *Best British Short Stories of 1932*, edited by Edward J. O'Brien. New York: Houghton Mifflin, 1933.

Novels

Clare Drummer. London: Ernest Benn, 1929.

Dead Man Leading. London: Chatto & Windus, 1937; New York: Macmillan, 1937. Reprint. New York: Oxford University Press, 1985.

Mr. Beluncle. London: Chatto & Windus, 1935; New York: Macmillan, 1935.

Nothing like Leather. London: Chatto & Windus, 1935; New York: Macmillan, 1935.

Shirley Sanz. London: Victor Gollancz, 1932. Republished as *Elopement into Exile*. Boston: Little, Brown, 1932.

Criticism

Balzac. London: Chatto & Windus, 1973; New York: Alfred A. Knopf, 1973.

Books in General. London: Chatto & Windus, 1953; New York: Harcourt, Brace, 1953. Reprint. Westport, Conn.: Greenwood Press, 1970.

Chekhov: A Spirit Set Free. London: Hodder and Stoughton, 1988; New York: Random House, 1988.

The Gentle Barbarian: The Life and Work of Turgenev. London: Chatto & Windus, 1977; New York: Random House, 1977.

George Meredith and English Comedy: The Clark Lectures for 1969. London: Chatto & Windus, 1970; New York: Random House, 1970.

In My Good Books. London: Chatto & Windus, 1942. Reprint. Port Washington, N.Y.: Kennicat Press, 1970.

Lasting Impressions. London: Chatto & Windus, 1990.

The Living Novel. London: Chatto & Windus, 1946. Revised Edition, *The Living Novel and Other Appreciations*. New York: Random House, 1964.

A Man of Letters. London: Chatto & Windus, 1985; New York: Random House, 1986.

The Myth Makers: Literary Essays. London: Chatto & Windus, 1979; New York: Random House, 1979.

Shakespeare: The Comprehensive Soul. London: British Broadcasting Corporation, 1965.

The Tale Bearers: Literary Essays. London: Chatto & Windus, 1980; New York: Random House, 1980.

Why Do I Write? (with Elizabeth Bowen and Graham Greene). London: Marshall, 1948.

The Working Novelist. London: Chatto & Windus, 1965; New York: Random House, 1965.

Travel

At Home and Abroad. Berkeley, Calif.: North Point Press, 1989.

Dublin: A Portrait. London: Bodley Head, 1967; New York: Harper & Row, 1967.

Foreign Faces. London: Chatto & Windus, 1964. Republished as *The Offensive Traveller.* New York: Alfred A. Knopf, 1964.

London Perceived. London: Chatto & Windus, 1962; New York: Harcourt, Brace & World, 1962.

Marching Spain. London: Ernest Benn, 1928.

New York Proclaimed. London: Chatto & Windus, 1965; New York: Harcourt, Brace & World, 1965.

The Spanish Temper. London: Chatto & Windus, 1954; New York: Alfred A. Knopf, 1955.

Omnibus

The Other Side of the Frontier: A V. S. Pritchett Reader. London: Robin Clark, 1984. The short stories are represented by "The Sailor," "Things as They Are," "Sense of Humour," "The Wheelbarrow," "The Fall," "When My Girl Comes Home," "A Debt of Honour," "The Diver," and "Did You Invite Me?"

Autobiography

"As Old as the Century." *Observer,* 14 December 1980, 23, 25. Republished as "Looking Back at 80." *New York Times Magazine,* 14 December 1980, 40+.

A Cab at the Door. London: Chatto & Windus, 1968; New York: Random House, 1968.

Midnight Oil. London: Chatto & Windus, 1971; New York: Random House, 1972.

The Turn of the Years. Wilton, U.K.: Michael Russell, 1981. Pritchett's essay "As Old as the Century" with engravings by Reynolds Stone and an introduction by Paul Theroux.

Edited Works

The Oxford Book of Short Stories. New York: Oxford University Press, 1981.

Robert Louis Stevenson, Novels and Stories. London: Pilot Press, 1945; New York: Duell, Sloan & Pearce, 1946.

This England. London: New Statesman & Nation, 1937.

Turnstile One: A Literary Miscellany from the New Statesman and Nation. London: Turnstile Press, 1948.

Essays on the Short Story

Introduction to *The Oxford Book of Short Stories*, chosen by V. S. Pritchett, xl–xlv. New York: Oxford University Press, 1981.

"The Writer's Tale." *Vogue,* March 1981, 327–28, 362.

"The Short Story" (with William Sansom and Francis King). *London Magazine,* September 1966, 6–12.

Secondary Sources

Interviews

Cassidy, Suzanne. "A Noticing Kind of Person." *New York Times Book Review,* 22 October 1989, 3.

Forkner, Ben, and Philippe Séjourné. "An Interview with V. S. Pritchett." *Journal of the Short Story in English* 6 (Spring 1986): 11–38.

Guppy, Shusha, and Anthony Weller. "The Art of Fiction CXXII: V. S. Pritchett." *Paris Review* 117 (Winter 1990): 182–207.

Haffenden, John. "V. S. Pritchett." In his *Novelists in Interview,* 210–30. London: Methuen, 1985.

Hughes, Douglas A. "V. S. Pritchett: An Interview." *Studies in Short Fiction* 13 (Fall 1976): 423–32.

Nichols, Lewis. "Talk with V. S. Pritchett." *New York Times Book Review,* 25 April 1954, 16.

Smith, Robert W. "Visiting with Sir Victor." *Washington Post Book World,* 18 November 1979, 1, 8–9.

"V. S. Pritchett." *Vogue,* March 1981, 326–28.

Books

Baldwin, Dean R. *V. S. Pritchett.* Boston: Twayne Publishers, 1987.

Theil, Alain. *Les Nouvelles de V. S. Pritchett.* Clermont-Ferrand: Association des publications de la faculte des lettres et sciences humaines, 1982.

Articles and Reviews

Abrahams, William. "Victor Victorious." Review of *Collected Stories. Harper's,* August 1982, 74–75.

Allen, Walter. "V. S. Pritchett." In his *The Short Story in English,* 268–75. New York: Oxford University Press, 1981.

Aquien, Pascal. " 'The Diver' or the Plunge into Fantasy." *Journal of the Short Story in*

English 6 (Spring 1986): 47–57.

Bailey, Anthony. "Puritan's Eye." Review of *The Sailor, Sense of Humour, and Other Stories*. *Commonweal*, 14 September 1956, 593–95.

Baro, Gene. "Meet Bob Fraser." Review of *The Key to My Heart*. *New York Times Book Review*, 15 November 1964, 5.

Binding, Paul. "A Kindly Art." Review of *The Complete Short Stories*. *New Statesman and Society*, 23 November 1990, 38.

Boston, Anne. "Storyteller's Glee." Review of *A Careless Widow and Other Stories*. *New Statesman and Society*, 25 August 1989, 28.

Broyard, Anatole. "The Ordinary People." *New York Times*, 24 April 1982, 18.

Core, George. "V. S. Pritchett and the Life of Art." Review of *The Myth Makers, On the Edge of the Cliff*, and *The Tale Bearers*. *Sewanee Review* 89 (Spring 1981): xxxviii, xl, xlii–xliii.

Crews, Frederick C. "Comedy and Beyond." Review of *The Key to My Heart*. *New York Review of Books*, 3 December 1964, 5.

Cunningham, Valentine. "Coping with the Bigger Words." Review of *Collected Stories*. *Times Literary Supplement*, 25 June 1982, 687.

———. "The Flesh-and-Bone Merchant." Review of *The Complete Short Stories*. *Times Literary Supplement*, 23 November 1990, 1255–56.

———. "Great Tipster." Review of *The Camberwell Beauty*. *Times Literary Supplement*, 25 October 1974, 1182.

Davenport, Guy. "Love Is Always Too Early and Never Too Late." Review of *Blind Love*. *New York Times Book Review*, 25 January 1970, 4.

Davies, Robertson. "V. S. Pritchett: Storyteller Supreme." *Washington Post Book World*, 25 April 1982, 1–2, 5.

DeMott, Benjamin. "Ironic Comedy." Review of *On the Edge of the Cliff*. *New York Times Book Review*, 18 November 1979, 1, 41–42.

Donoghue, Denis. "The Uncompleted Dossier." Review of *Blind Love*. *New York Review of Books*, 12 March 1970, 27.

Doze, Geneviève. "Two Tentative Readings of 'Many Are Disappointed.' " *Journal of the Short Story in English* 6 (Spring 1986): 59–66.

"English Eccentrics." Review of *The Key to My Heart*. *Times Literary Supplement*, 25 October 1963, 847.

Furbank, P. N. "The Professional Touch." Review of *A Careless Widow and Other Stories*. *Times Literary Supplement*, 25 August 1989, 917.

Glendenning, Victoria. "Playing Charades." Review of *On the Edge of the Cliff*. *Times Literary Supplement*, 29 February 1980, 228.

Hanson, Clare. *Short Stories and Short Fictions, 1880–1980*. New York: St. Martin's, 1980.

Heath, Susan. Review of *The Camberwell Beauty*. *Saturday Review/World*, 19 October

1974, 28–29.

Hodgart, Matthew. Review of *The Camberwell Beauty and Other Stories*. *New York Review of Books*, 20 March 1975, 32.

Howe, Irving. "Tales of Weary England." Review of *The Sailor, Sense of Humour, and Other Stories*. *New Republic*, 17 September 1956, 18.

Hughes, Douglas A. "The Eclipsing of V. S. Pritchett and H. E. Bates: A Representative Case of Critical Myopia." *Studies in Short Fiction* 19 (Fall 1982): iii–iv.

———. Review of *Collected Stories*. *Studies in Short Fiction* 20 (Spring–Summer 1983): 139–40.

———. Review of *On the Edge of the Cliff*. *Studies in Short Fiction* 17 (Summer 1980): 355–56.

Jones, D. A. N. "Laments for Other People." Review of *The Camberwell Beauty*. *Times Literary Supplement*, 25 October 1974, 1182.

Kakutani, Michiko. "Gentle Illuminations." Review of *More Collected Stories*. *New York Times Book Review*, September 1983, 11.

———. "A V. S. Pritchett Collection of Characters." Review of *A Careless Widow and Other Stories*. *New York Times*, 6 October 1989, C29.

Kermode, Frank. "A Century of Stories." Review of *Complete Collected Stories*. *New York Times Book Review*, 24 March 1991, 1, 28–29.

Kiely, Robert. "A Writer Who Trusts His Readers." Review of *Collected Stories*. *New York Times Book Review*, 30 May 1982, 5–6.

Larrière, Claire. "Explosions and Catharses." *Journal of the Short Story in English* 6 (Spring 1986): 67–74.

Lee, Hermione. "Boasters on Their Dangerous Journeys." *Times Literary Supplement*, 4 November 1983, 1214.

Leiter, Robert. Review of *More Collected Stories*. *America*, 31 December 1983, 437–38.

"Life's Inconsequences." Review of *You Make Your Own Life*. *Times Literary Supplement*, 5 February 1938, 91.

Lohafer, Susan. " 'The Wheelbarrow' by V. S. Pritchett." In *Coming to Terms with the Short Story*, 148–53. Baton Rouge: Louisiana State University Press, 1983.

Magid, Nora L. "Blind Love and Other Stories." *Commonweal*, 15 May 1970, 227–29.

Marks, Harry S. "V. S. Pritchett." *Dictionary of Literary Biography* 15: 464–71. Detroit: Gale Research, 1983.

Mayne, Richard. "Keep Britain Untidy." Review of *When My Girl Comes Home*. *New Statesman*, 13 October 1961, 526.

Mellors, John. "V. S. Pritchett: Man on the Other Side of a Frontier." *London Magazine*, April/May 1975, 5–13.

Moore, Lorrie. Review of *A Careless Widow and Other Stories*. *New York Times Book Review*, 22 October 1989, 3.

Morris, Robert K. "He Thinks People Are Human." Review of *The Camberwell Beauty*. *Nation*, 10 May 1975, 570–72.

Mortimer, Penelope. Review of *The Camberwell Beauty*. *New York Times Book Review*, 15 September 1974, 31.

Oumhani, Cécile. "Water in V. S. Pritchett's Art of Revealing." *Journal of the Short Story in English* 6 (Spring 1986): 75–91.

Peden, William. "Realism and Anti-realism in the Modern Short Story." In *The Teller and the Tale: Aspects of the Short Story*, edited by Wendell M. Aycock, 47–62. Lubbock: Texas Tech Press, 1982.

———. Review of *Blind Love*. *Saturday Review*, 14 March 1970, 39–40.

———. "V. S. Pritchett." In *The English Short Story, 1880–1945*, edited by Joseph M. Flora, 143–51. Boston: Twayne Publishers, 1985.

Penner, Jonathan. "Glimpses of Illicit Love." Review of *On the Edge of the Cliff*. *Washington Post Book World*, 18 November 1979, 1–9.

Pouillard, Michel. "V. S. Pritchett's 'The Aristocrat' as a One-Act Comedy." *Journal of the Short Story in English* 6 (Spring 1986): 93–100.

Prawer, S. S. "The Soul of Beauty." Review of *Collected Stories* and *The Other Side of the Frontier*. *Times Literary Supplement*, 17 August 1984, 926.

Raban, Jonathan. "Going Strong." Review of *Collected Stories* and *The Turn of the Years: As Old as the Century*. *New York Review of Books*, 24 June 1982, 8–10.

Schwartz, Lynne Sharon. "V. S. Pritchett's Stories of Craft and Cunning." *Washington Post Book World*, 9 October 1983, 5.

Scott-James, R. A. "The Five Mr. Pritchetts." *New Republic*, 20 August 1956, 18.

Sheed, Wilfrid. "Racing the Clock with Greene and Pritchett." Review of *Travels with My Aunt* and *Blind Love*. *Atlantic*, April 1970, 109–13.

Sheppard, R.Z. "A Clarity of Mind, a Clarity of Heart." Review of *On the Edge of the Cliff*. *Time*, 12 November 1979, 127.

Sigal, Clancy. "Low Lifemanship." *The Listener*, 5 August 1982, 22–23.

"The Temptations of a Technique." Review of *When My Girl Comes Home*. *Times Literary Supplement*, 6 October 1961, 657.

Theil, Alain. "V. S. Pritchett's Quiet Expressionism." *Journal of the Short Story in English* 6 (Spring 1986): 101–10.

Theroux, Paul. "V. S. Pritchett's Stories: His Greatest Triumph." Review of *Collected Stories*. *Saturday Review*, May 1982, 56–57.

Towers, Robert. "Fair Play." Review of *On the Edge of the Cliff*. *New York Review of Books*, 7 February 1980, 25.

Trevor, William. "Pritchett Proclaimed." Review of *Collected Stories*. *New Republic*, 2 August 1982, 30–32.

Vannatta, Dennis, ed. *The English Short Story 1945–1980*. Boston: Twayne Publishers, 1985.

_____ . "V. S. Pritchett." In *Critical Survey of Short Fiction* 6, edited Frank N. Magill, 2128–33. Englewood Cliffs, N.J.: Salem Press, 1981.

Vickery, John, and J'nan M. Sellery, eds. "Ritual in the Streets: A Study of Pritchett's 'The Scapegoat.' " In their *Ritual and Literature*, 226–37. Boston: Houghton Mifflin, 1972.

Welty, Eudora. "A Family of Emotions." Review of *Selected Stories. New York Times Book Review*, 25 June 1978, 1, 39–40.

Yvard, Pierre. "V. S. Pritchett and the Short Narrative in 'The Fly in the Ointment.' " *Journal of the Short Story in English* 6 (Spring 1986): 111–21.

Index

Abbey Theatre, xiii
"The Accompanist," 64–66, 75
allegory, 12, 55, 59, 76; political, 14, 15
Allen, Walter, xii, 3; *The Short Story in English* 108, 108(n2), 121(n2); "V. S. Pritchett," xiv, xiv(n6), xv, xvii(n6)
"The Ape," 76
Aquien, Pascal, "'The Diver' or the Plunge into Fantasy," 61, 61(n28), 85(n28)
"The Aristocrat," 17
Atlantic, 63
"Aunt Gertrude," 20
Auden, W. H., 100
Austen, Jane, 98, 129
autobiography, V. S. Pritchett, 20–21, 90, 95, 98

Babel, Isaak, xiv, 21, 93
Baldwin, Dean R., *V. S. Pritchett*, xi, xii, 8, 8(n5), 15, 58–59, 84(n5)
Baroja, Pio, xiv
Barrie, J. M., *When a Man's Single*, 81–82
Barthes, Roland, xi
Bates, H. E., xi, xiv, 92; "The Mill," 104
Bayley, John, *The Short Story*, 77–78, 78(n30), 85(n30)
Bellow, Saul, 104
Bergler, Edmund, 10
Binding, Paul, "A Kindly Art," 8, 8(n6), 84(n6)
black comedy, 6

"Blind Love," 48, 49–51, 60, 75, 99, 113–15, 123
Blind Love, 48–54, 73, 75, 85(n29)
Bowen, Elizabeth, stories, 104
Britannia, 76
British humorists, disappearance of, 104
British television, Pritchett story filmed for, 67
Broyard, Anatole: "Ah, Sweet Mystery of Life," 58, 58(n26), 85(n26); "On the Edge of the Cliff," 3, 3(n1), 84(n1)
Burgess, Anthony, 89

A Cab at the Door, xii, 21, 82, 82(n33), 85(n33), 90
"The Cage Birds," 48, 52–53, 74, 82
"The Camberwell Beauty," 3, 55–57, 73, 75, 125–26
The Camberwell Beauty, 55–62, 73, 74, 75, 85(n29), 90
"A Careless Widow," 53, 70, 75, 83
A Careless Widow, 55, 73, 75, 85(n29), 119(n5), 121(n5)
"The Chain-Smoker," 73–74
"A Change of Policy," 70–71, 75
Chatterly, Sir Clifford, 16
Chatto & Windus, publishers, 36
Chekhov, Anton, xiv, 29, 48, 79, 81, 92, 94, 103, 130
Chesterton, G. K., xiv, 98
"The Chestnut Tree," 20, 24, 73
Christian Science, xii, 34, 82
Christian Science Monitor, Pritchett as correspondent for, xiii

"The Citizen," 76
Clare Drummer, xiii
class comedies, 74
"The Clerk's Tale," 20, 73
Collected Stories, 17, 19, 36, 55,
    109(n4), 121(n4); preface to, 4,
    4(n3), 17, 18, 20, 21, 84(n3), 127
"The Collection," 36
"Cocky Olly," 69–70, 73
comic irony, 25, 26, 44
Complete Collected Stories, xiv, xv, 3, 5,
    17, 18
Conrad, Joseph, as "finest English
    short story writer," 104
Coppard, A. E., xi, xiv, 129
Cornwall, 83, 99
"The Cuckoo Clock," 17, 20, 74
Cunningham, Valentine, review of
    Collected Stories, xv(n8),
    xvi(n8)

Davie, Elspeth, 104
Davies, Robertson, 3; "V. S. Pritchett:
    Storyteller Supreme," 40(n20),
    85(n20)
"Debt of Honor," 48
de la Mare, Walter, 129
"Did You Invite Me?", 55, 62, 75
Dickens, Charles, xiv, 22, 30, 81, 93,
    103; *David Copperfield*, xii;
    Dickensian influence on
    Pritchett, 95; *Household Words*,
    95
"The Diver" ("The Fall"), 55, 59–61,
    64, 73, 82, 109–10, 122–23
Dostoevsky, Feodor, 98
"Double Divan," 36
Doze, Geneviève, "Two Tentative
    Readings of 'Many Are
    Disappointed,'" 28(n15),
    84(n15)
Drabble, Margaret, 3
Duffy, James (one of Joyce's

Dubliners), 68

Edwardian world, 75
"Eleven O'clock," 15–16, 75
Eliot, George (Mary Ann Evans), 93
Encounter, 55, 63
England and the short story, 129;
    North-South contrast in
    Pritchett stories, 16
English short stories, Pritchett's
    opinion on, 104
Enright, D. J., 103
Eros, 64, 79, 109, 115, 116
Evans, Caradoc, 44

"The Fall," 45–46
"A Family Man," 75
"The Fig Tree," 64, 66, 75
Fitzgerald, F. Scott, 4
Flaubert, Gustave, 98
"The Fly in the Ointment," 20, 82
folktale(s), 14
Forkner, Ben, and Philippe Séjourné,
    "An Interview with V. S.
    Pritchett," 21, 21(n14), 26, 67,
    68, 73, 77, 78, 80, 84(n14)
Fowles, John, *The Collector*, 57
France, Anatole, xiv; as influence on
    Pritchett, 98
Fuller, Roy, 103

Gallant, Mavis, 104
Gibbon, Edward, *The History of the
    Decline and Fall of the Roman
    Empire*, 101
Gordimer, Nadine, 104
Guppy, Shusha, and Anthony
    Weller: "The Art of Fiction
    CXXII: V. S. Pritchett,"
    19(n13), 31, 84(n13)

Haffenden, John, "V. S. Pritchett,"
    8–9(n7), 41, 48, 79, 84(n7)

"Handsome Is as Handsome Does,"
8–11, 19, 46, 49, 74, 75, 129–30
Hardy, Thomas, 93
Harper's, 48
Heath, Susan, review of *The
Camberwell Beauty*, xii(n3),
xv(n3)
Heller, Joseph, *Catch-22*, 15
Hemingway, Ernest, as influence on
Pritchett, xiv, 4, 11, 80, 98, 99,
103
Hester Prynne, 59
Hill, Susan, 104
Hodgart, Matthew, review of *The
Camberwell Beauty*, xii(n2),
xv(n2)
homosexual(s), 67, 68
Hughes, Douglas A., "V. S. Pritchett,
an Interview," xiv(n4), xv,
xv(n4), 12(n10), 84(n10), 89,
90–101, 109(n3), 121(n3); guest
editorial in *Studies in Short
Fiction*, 107; essay on V. S.
Pritchett, 108–21

"The Image Trade," 71–72
impressionist painting, xiv
Ireland and the short story, 94, 129
irony in modern literature, 4
Italians and the short story, 94
"It May Never Happen," xiv, 3, 19,
20, 21–24, 27, 73, 74, 76, 78, 82
It May Never Happen, 19–36, 40, 73,
74, 75, 76, 85(n29)

James, Henry, 37, 66; *What Maisie
Knew*, 26
Jhabvala, Ruth Prawer, 104
Joyce, James, xiv, 92, 97, 98, 108, 128,
130; influence on V. S.
Pritchett, 96, 97; *Dubliners*, 53,
68, 96, 128; *Finnegans Wake*,
128; "A Painful Case," 67;

Ulysses, 96, 128
"Just a Little More," 82

Kermode, Frank, xii, 3
"The Key to My Heart," 46, 74
The Key to My Heart, 46–48, 74, 75,
85(n29)
Kipling, Rudyard, 93, 103, 104, 129;
"Mary Postgate," 103; as
"finest English writer," 104
Knopf, Alfred A., Inc., publishers, 36

"The Ladder," 36, 38–39, 75
"Lady from Guatemala," 55, 61–62,
75
"The Landlord," 36, 37–38, 74, 75
Lardner, Ring, "Haircut," 11
Larkin, Philip, 103
"Last Throw," 55, 74
Lavin, Mary, xi, 92, 94, 97
Lawrence, D. H., xiv, xv, 31, 44, 67,
103, 112, 128, 129; as "finest
English short story writer,"
104; "The Blind Man," 51;
"The Horse Dealer's
Daughter," 51; "The Man
Who Loved Islands," 128;
"The Rocking-Horse Winner,"
128
Lessing, Doris, 104
Lewis, Sinclair, 5
"The Liars," 48, 73
"The Lion's Den," 20, 82
literary art, 71
literature, function of, 98
Lohafer, Susan, " 'The Wheelbarrow'
by V. S. Pritchett," 43–44,
44(n22), 85(n22)
London Mercury, 15
London Perceived, 55–56, 56(n25),
85(n25)
love stories, V. S. Pritchett's, 48,
49–52, 122–26

Low, David, 69; Colonel Blimp, 69

McEwan, Ian, 104
"Main Road," 15, 76
Manning, Olivia, 104
Mansfield, Katherine, xiv
"Many Are Disappointed," 28–29,
    99, 128–29
Marching Spain, xiii
"The Marvellous Girl," 55, 57–59, 75,
    123–24
Maugham, Somerset, 104, 129
Maupassant, Guy de, xiv, 17, 91, 92,
    104
Mellors, John, "V. S. Pritchett: Man
    on the Other Side of a
    Frontier," xii(n1), xv(n1)
Meredith, George, 41
Middlemarch, 91
Midnight Oil, xii, 4, 4(n4), 5, 20, 21,
    30, 52, 59, 78, 82, 84(n4), 90,
    100
Mr. Beluncle, 24, 40
Modern literary theory, 78
Moore, George, "Celibates," 104
More Collected Stories, 17, 25
Murdoch, Iris, 57
myth, 59

Naipaul, V. S., 104
nationality and the short story, 94,
    129
"The Nest Builder," 48, 51–52, 53–54,
    75
"New Criticism, xii,
New Statesman, 40, 63, 90; Pritchett's
    editorial work for, 40
New Yorker, 46, 47, 48, 55, 63, 90
New York Review of Books, 90
Nietzche, Friedrich, 98
"The Night Worker," 20, 25–26
"Noisy Flushes the Birds," 46, 74
"Noisy in the Doghouse," 46, 74

North-South of England, contrast in
    Pritchett stories, 16
Nothing like Leather, 21

O'Brien, Edna, 104
O'Brien, Edward J., 17; *Best Short
    Stories of the Year*, 17, 18
O'Casey, Sean, xiii
O'Connor, Frank, 92, 103; as short
    story critic, 94; "Guests of the
    Nation," 103; *The Lonely Voice*,
    75
"The Oedipus Complex," 22, 26–27
O'Faolain, Sean, 92, 97
O'Flaherty, Liam, xiv, 97, 103
O. Henry (William Sydney Porter),
    104
"On the Edge of the Cliff," 63–64, 75,
    79, 83, 103, 117–18
On the Edge of the Cliff, 55, 62–67, 74,
    75, 85(n29), 128
Oumhani, Cecile, "Water in V. S.
    Pritchett's Art of Revealing,"
    60, 60(n27), 85(n27)
"Our Wife" ("The Captain's
    Daughter"), 55, 58, 75
The Oxford Book of Short Stories,
    29(n16), 77; intro duction to,
    29(n16), 77, 84(n16)

"Page and Monarch," 73
"Passing the Ball," 36, 37, 74
Peden, William, "*Blind Love*,"
    54(n24), 85(n24); "Realism and
    Anti-realism," 11, 11(n9),
    84(n9); "V. S. Pritchett," xiv,
    xv(n5), 10, 10(n8), 84(n8)
Penner, Jonathan:, "Glimpses of
    Illicit Love," 79(n32), 85(n32)
Pinter, Harold, 29
Playboy, 55, 63
"Pocock Passes," 27–28, 43
Poe, Edgar Allan, 92

Polhemus, Robert M., *Comic Faith:
The Great Tradition from Austen
to Joyce*, 108(n1), 121(n1)
Pritchett, Beatrice Martin (mother),
xii, xiii
Pritchett, Dorothy Roberts (wife),
xiii, 89
Pritchett, Walter Sawdon (father), xii,
22, 76, 82; as prototype of
Pritchett characters, xiii, 82

Queen, 48

Random House, publishers, 46
"The Rescue," 55, 59, 73, 74
Roberts, Kate, 31
Russia and the short story, 94, 129
Russian novels, 4
Russian writers, 103

"The Sack of Lights," 76
"The Sailor," xiv, 19, 27, 29–34, 36,
40, 43, 74, 75, 76, 78, 82, 103
The Sailor, Sense of Humour, 36–39, 74,
75; preface to, 19(n12), 20, 74,
81, 84(n12), 85(n29), 90
"The Saint," xiv, 19, 20, 29, 34–36, 73,
79, 82
Sansom, William, "Fireman Flower,"
104
satire, 11, 108
"The Satisfactory," 36, 37
"The Scapegoat," 14–15, 76
Scott, Sir Walter, "The Two
Drovers," 104
Séjourné, Philippe, 21, 21(n14),
84(n14)
Selected Stories, 17
"Sense of Humour," xiv, 3, 4–8, 18,
19, 73, 76–78, 79, 82, 98–99
"Short Stories," 78(n31), 85(n31)
short story: American, 94, 129; art of,
77, 89, 127; flourishing in

anarchic societies, 94;
implicitness in, 4; indirection
in, 4; intensity of, 91; like a
lyric poem, 92; nationality
and, 94, 129; neglect of the
genre, 91, 92, 93;
suggestiveness in, 4; revision
of, 93; theory of, 24; twentieth-
century, 4; vs. the novel, 102–3
"The Short Story," 40, 40(n19),
85(n19)
Sillitoe, Alan, "The Loneliness of the
Long-Distance Runner," 103
"The Skeleton," 48, 53–54, 64, 115–17,
125
Slavonic Jews and the short story, 94
Smith, Robert W., "Visiting with Sir
Victor," 29(n17), 84(n17)
"The Sniff," 36, 76
social comedy, 46, 75
social protest, 15, 76
social realism, 5
Spain, Pritchett's first travel book on,
xiii, 129
"The Spanish Virgin," 20
The Spanish Virgin, xiii, 17, 73, 74, 76,
85(n29)
Spark, Muriel, 104
"The Speech," 48
spiritual isolation, 73
"The Spree," 55, 61, 75, 118–19, 122
"A Spring Morning," 16–17, 75
Stein, Gertrude, 4
Sterne, Laurence, 80
Stevenson, Robert Louis, xiv, 98, 104;
as influence on Pritchett, 98
"A Story of Don Juan," 36
stream-of-consciousness, 76
Studies in Short Fiction, 107
symbolism, 59
Synge, J. M., *The Playboy of the
Western World*, 15

"Tea with Mrs. Bittell," 75, 76
"The Temptation of a Technique,"
40, 40(n21), 85(n21)
Thanatos, 64
Theil, Alain, *Les Nouvelles de V. S.
Pritchett*, xi
Theroux, Paul, xii, xiv, 3, 104; "V. S.
Pritchett's Stories: His
Greatest Triumph," xiv(n7),
xvi(n7)
"Things as They Are," 36, 37, 104
Times Literary Supplement, 17; review
of Pritchett's *When My Girl
Comes Home*, 40, 40(n21),
85(n21)
Todorov, Tzvetan, xi
Tolstoy, Leo, 98; *War and Peace*, 91
tragedy, 11
"Tragedy in a Greek Theatre," 17
Trevor, William, xi, xiv, xv, 3, 107;
"Attracta," 104; "Pritchett
Proclaimed," 127–30
"A Trip to the Seaside," 75, 118,
119–21
"The Two Brothers," 76
Twohy, Frank, 104
Turgenev, Ivan, 92, 94
*The Turn of the Years: As Old as the
Century*, 82–83, 83(n34),
85(n34), 89, 89(n1)

"The Upright Man," 12–14, 73, 75–76

Valéry, Paul, *Analects*, introduction
to, 100, 101
Vickery, John, and J'nan M. Sellery,
"Ritual in the Streets," 14–15,
15(n11), 84(n11)

warfare, modern, 12
war, relationship to work, 12
Warner, Sylvia Townsend, xi, xiv, 47
Waugh, Evelyn, 47
"The Wedding," 66–67, 75, 112–13
Wells, H. G., xiv
Welty, Eudora, xv, 3, 107, 109; "A
Family of Emotions," 83,
83(n35), 85(n35), 122–26
"The Wheelbarrow," 43–45, 110–12
"When My Girl Comes Home," 3, 4,
40–43, 73, 76, 124–25
When My Girl Comes Home, 40–46, 73,
76, 85(n29)
"The White Rabbit," 17, 73
Williams, Michael, "Welsh Voices in
the Short Story," 44(n23),
85(n23)
Wilson, Angus, xiv, 47
Wodehouse, P. G., 47; as poet in his
comedies, 103
Woolf, Virginia, xiv
work, dehumanizing nature of, 12
World War I, literature about, 13–14
"The Worshippers," 74
Wright, Austin M., "Recalcitrance in
the Short Story," 4, 4(n2),
84(n2)
"The Writer's Tale," xv, 31(n18),
84(n18), 89, 102–4

Yeats, William Butler, xiii
"You Make Your Own Life," 11–12,
19, 75, 76
You Make Your Own Life, 8–18, 19, 20,
36, 73, 74, 75, 76, 85(n29)

The Author

John Stinson is professor of English at SUNY College at Fredonia, where he joined the faculty in 1965. He has taught a wide variety of courses, but his specialty is modern British literature. He received his Ph.D in English from New York University in 1971. He is the author of *Anthony Burgess Revisited*, published in 1991 as part of Twayne's English Authors Series, and a contributor to the Twayne volume *The English Short Story, 1945–1980*. In addition to several articles on Anthony Burgess, he has published in various academic journals essays on William Golding, Graham Greene, David Storey, William Trevor, and Arthur Miller.

The Editor

General editor Gordon Weaver earned his B.A. in English at the University of Wisconsin-Milwaukee in 1961; his M.A. in English at the University of Illinois, where he studied as a Woodrow Wilson Fellow, in 1962; and his Ph.D. in English and creative writing at the University of Denver in 1970. His novels include *Count a Lonely Cadence, Give Him a Stone, Circling Byzantium,* and *The Eight Corners of the World.* Many of his short stories are collected in *The Entombed Man of Thule, Such Waltzing Was Not Easy, Getting Serious, Morality Play, A World Quite Round,* and *Men Who Would Be Good.* He edited *The American Short Story, 1945-1980: A Critical History,* and is currently editor of *Cimarron Review.* He is professor of English at Oklahoma State University and serves as an adjunct member of the faculty of the Vermont College Master of Fine Arts in Writing Program.